Ti̇̀...
A
to ge... ...
Looking forward to
ongoing conversation
& collaboration

Mal

MORE PRAISE FOR
The Moment You Can't Ignore

"The authors bring to life the importance of culture: how very different it is from other elements of change management and how critical it is to take advantage of 'un-ignorable moments.' Their stories are compelling and memorable."—Jon Katzenbach, Senior Executive Advisor, the Katzenbach Center, coauthor of *The Wisdom of Team*, and coauthor (with Zia Khan) of *Leading Outside the Lines*

"*The Moment You Can't Ignore* brings us something we have not seen in a long time—a new set of ideas for leaders managing complex and continually changing organizations. This book provides vivid examples of how leaders can create 'superconducting organizations' capable of successfully managing the rip tides of change that threaten organizational identity, clarity about who is charge, and confidence that they can both adapt to and shape their future. Doing so requires the ability to know and leverage the moments in your organization you can't ignore. This book is a roadmap to being able to identify and leverage those moments."—David Thomas, Dean and William R. Berkley Chair of Georgetown University's McDonough School of Business, and coauthor of *Breaking Through: The Making of Minority Executives in Corporate America*

The Moment
You Can't Ignore

The Moment You Can't Ignore

WHEN **BIG TROUBLE** LEADS
TO A **GREAT FUTURE**

*How Culture
Drives Strategic Change*

**Malachi O'Connor
and Barry Dornfeld**

PublicAffairs
New York

Published in the United States by PublicAffairs™, a Member of the
Perseus Books Group

PublicAffairs books are available at special discounts for bulk purchases
in the U.S. by corporations, institutions, and other organizations. For more
information, please contact the Special Markets Department at the Perseus
Books Group, 2300 Chestnut Street, Suite 200, Philadelphia, PA 19103,
call (800) 810-4145, ext. 5000, or e-mail special.markets@perseusbooks
.com.

Book Design by Pauline Brown

Library of Congress Cataloging-in-Publication Data
O'Connor, Malachi.
The moment you can't ignore : when big trouble leads to a great future /
Malachi O'Connor and Barry Dornfeld.
pages cm
Includes bibliographical references and index.
ISBN 978–1-61039–465–9 (hardback)—ISBN 978–1-61039–466–6
(ebook) 1. Corporate culture. 2. Organizational behavior. 3. Organizational
change. 4. Leadership. I. Dornfeld, Barry, 1958-II. Title.
HD58.7.O244 2014
658.4'06—dc23
2014023886

First Edition

10 9 8 7 6 5 4 3 2 1

To each of our wives,
Bonnie O'Connor and Carole Boughter—
thank you for thirty years
of love, inspiration, partnership,
and for helping us through
our own un-ignorable moments.

CONTENTS

Introduction

The Many Ways to Attend a Funeral

W E FIRST ENCOUNTERED A MOMENT we could not ignore almost thirty years ago—at the funeral of a Hmong friend named Bee Lor. We weren't in the highlands of southern China where the Hmong originated, or in Laos where they lived in refugee camps after fighting for the United States during the Vietnam War. We were in Philadelphia, Pennsylvania, where the Hmong had immigrated in the 1970s—a place as familiar to us as it was unfamiliar to the Hmong.

At the time, we knew the funeral was an important moment but had no idea how important it would become for us today as we work with company after company facing challenges that are cultural at their core. In those Philadelphia days, we were training as ethnographers and just beginning to explore how culture works. Today, when we listen to people talk about the problems they are having with "culture," we know what they really mean: *Our organization is stuck. We're not quite sure how or why. Or what to do about it.*

The problem of organizations getting stuck has intensified in the past decade. As continuous change became the new normal, addressing cultural challenges became more difficult. Each wave of change was followed by another, bringing with it a demand for new capabilities, new ways of working, new behaviors. People had no time to catch their breath, reflect, and assess where they were.

As organizational change came crashing in, it encountered resistance. Increasing friction brought issues of culture to the attention of business leaders and challenged their ability to move their companies forward. While working with our clients, we began hearing phrases like "culture eats strategy for lunch," an aphorism often attributed to management thinker Peter Drucker. It means that no matter how sharp or differentiated your strategy, if you do not have an organizational culture that can put this strategy into action it will likely fail.

When the stress of change becomes too much for an organization, the situation often erupts into an "un-ignorable moment"— an event or action, or even a comment, that stops you and your organization in its tracks, a moment when it becomes blindingly clear that new ways of working are clashing with existing ones. Paradoxically perhaps, the way to reduce the friction caused by these new ways of working can usually be found somewhere in the existing culture, which has the potential to be the most useful, resilient, and adaptable resource you have. But understanding that can take time. We've been learning about how culture works for some thirty years—ever since Bee Lor's funeral.

The un-ignorable moment that day provided an important lesson for us. At the time, we were working toward our doctoral degrees at the University of Pennsylvania—Barry at the Annenberg School for Communication and Mal in the Department of Folklore and Folklife. Not far from the Penn campus, a few thousand Hmong people lived in a refugee community, a cluster of rental homes in West Philadelphia. We met many of them, including Bee Lor, while working on a project to document the experiences of the Hmong.[1] They had migrated to the United States in the aftermath of the Vietnam War, settled in Philadelphia and other American cities, and gradually established a community. As a result of our work together, the Hmong came to know us as "American friends."

When we first worked with Bee, he was in his late teens. In his mid-twenties he was diagnosed with hepatitis B but led a pretty normal life for many years. He completed his education, got married, and started a family. In his late thirties, however, he suffered complications and, after a protracted illness, died.[2]

We were invited to a gathering that turned out to be similar to a Catholic wake. Bee had been laid out in a casket in the auditorium of the local high school. He was smartly dressed in a suit and his head rested on beautifully embroidered "sun pillows." There were hundreds of people there and we got in line to approach the casket and pay our respects.

That's when the un-ignorable moment arrived. The first mourner stepped forward, looked at Bee, and erupted in a wild outburst of emotion. She screamed. Threw up her hands. Fell across the casket. Sobbed uncontrollably. Then, just as suddenly as the outburst began, it stopped. She composed herself and moved on to the reception. Surely this was an anomaly? No. The next mourner stepped forward and did the same thing. And on it went. When our turn came, our somber looks and quiet demeanor seemed inappropriate and we felt awkward and weird.

What we had witnessed, of course, was an example of ritual mourning, a long-standing tradition in most cultures, but a version of mourning very different from what we had grown up with. At that funeral gathering, we saw that culture was not something that "others" who are "different" have. We understood that what seems natural and normal is largely defined by culture, by the perspectives we learn and bring to the world.

Now, when working with organizations, we encourage people to explore this point of view. When trying to make an organizational change, we are challenged to see our own culture clearly. And to do so, we have to find a way to "make the familiar strange" as the well-known anthropologist Ray Birdwhistell put it.[3] Only then can we identify what's causing big trouble and determine where our successful future lies.

EXPERIENCING AN UN-IGNORABLE MOMENT provides a superb opportunity to learn from that experience and take action, and that's where the method we were trained in, ethnography, can play a useful role. Ethnography studies culture by observing it in action. You can use what you learn to understand how your culture best adapts to change, without abandoning or violating its identity.

By using the ethnographic approach ("ethno" means "people or culture") you can understand the world in which a group of people live by seeing things through their eyes—or, as anthropologist Bronislaw Malinowski described it, taking "the native's point of view."[4] "Participant observation," a way of working at the heart of the ethnographic method, is particularly effective in organizations. It involves working and sometimes living with the people being studied. You engage with them in their own environment, participate in their activities, and ask them questions to strengthen your understanding.[5]

Ethnographic methods work as well on the front line, or in the boardroom, of a Fortune 500 company as they do with a refugee community in a city, if a little differently.[6] As social scientists, we seek understanding to deepen our knowledge about society or aid social change, while in business our goal is to improve performance by solving a specific problem that will lead to a positive change for the organization. For example, a software company might look at the work flow of its engineers to help them improve their efficiency. Retailers might study how consumers use their products in order to improve their offerings. We are not the only ones who have harnessed the power of ethnographic methods for improving business performance. Large companies such as 3M, Intel, and IBM, as well as smaller businesses and nonprofit organizations, have incorporated elements of the ethnographic approach in their quest for innovation.

When you observe people's behaviors in getting work done, you see that many of them are not formally defined but are tacit: not openly spoken about, although generally understood. Others are explicit: openly stated, shared, and discussed. An ethnographic perspective on organizational culture focuses on both:

- *Systemic agreements about how work gets done.* Work is conducted in organizations by following tacit as well as explicit agreements about how to divide tasks, how decisions should be made, and how to allocate and consume resources. When you are trying to make a change, these agreements, especially when they have become tacit and assumed to be "the way things get done around here," may become invalid. When that happens, people will no longer understand how to get their work done and productivity will plunge.

- *Rules for how individuals interact with one another.* There are many unspoken rules that pertain to human interaction. How to act in a meeting. How to communicate with a boss. How to work in teams. Again, when you are seeking change, these rules for interaction may no longer make sense. As a result, people will be unsure how to interact with others. They may be confused and hesitant. Conflicts may erupt and productivity will suffer.

Together, these two dimensions of culture play out in workplaces every day.

Four Questions That an Understanding of Culture Can Answer

When you seek to make a change or accomplish a transformation in your business, you need to pay attention to your organizational culture, understand it, and, very importantly, *trust* it. When you understand culture, you can answer four questions that are fundamental to any change effort:

- *What is our identity as an organization?* If you have gone through multiple shifts in strategy or a number of restructurings, your people may no longer be sure about the identity of the company. Who are we? What do we stand for? What's the connection between our identity and our strategy? These questions are as fundamental to your success as strategy-related questions, like, what business are we really in? When your people are uncertain about the company's identity, they will find it difficult to execute on any strategy with passion or commitment.
- *Who's in charge?* Sometimes people are not clear about who's in charge of any given initiative at any given time.

Is it the person with the title or the one with the expertise? Is it the maverick team leader or the unit executive? When people don't know who's in charge or how to determine who is in charge or should be, they may become paralyzed and unable to take action.

- *How do I lead?* People with formal authority may find themselves unable to lead effectively. Simply ordering others to follow them doesn't work—they don't know how to generate energy and spark enthusiasm for an idea or initiative. Although people in senior positions in traditional command-and-control hierarchies may realize they have to think about leadership differently, they may find it difficult to adjust to the emerging approach that we call "command and collaboration."

- *What is our future?* When people are unsure of what their company identity is, don't know who's in charge, and can't get behind their leaders, they have little capacity to innovate, make changes, and propel their organization forward. Old ideas get rehashed. New ideas get squashed or lost. Consequently, people are unable to navigate through the turbulent waters of the constantly changing business environment.

In this book, we take you on a journey that will help you answer these questions for your own organization. Why are these questions so important? Because they are the ones that always come up as a company struggles with change. Your problem may look unique to you but is likely a manifestation of the overarching issue that so many organizations are dealing with today: the organization as we have known it for decades is just not equipped to meet the challenges of working amid rapid and continuous change.

In the following chapters we present a method, developed over a period of years with companies of many kinds, that enables you to remove the barriers to success and make room for the capabilities needed to thrive and even transform a business. The ultimate goal is to become what we call a "superconducting" organization, in which:

- *Strategy and culture fuel each other.* Leaders continually translate strategy into specific, well-defined, on-the-ground actions and behaviors.
- *Hidden assets are leveraged.* Leaders value the courage of people throughout the organization, so hidden or underused assets are acknowledged, brought forward, and can be used effectively by others.
- *Interests are negotiated openly.* People hold honest, challenging conversations, negotiate their interests openly, and are supported in doing so. Agendas are made explicit, and people can see when and how their contributions have power.
- *Decision-making takes behavior into account.* When people make difficult decisions, they consider the impact of those decisions on behavior, so that people are clear about what to do and have the ability to learn from errors and make adjustments quickly.

These organizational features may sound simple and straight-forward, but can be quite difficult to achieve and sustain.

PREVIEW OF THE BOOK

The book unfolds in seven chapters. Three of them take the form of extended case narratives. They are based on real companies and their challenges, but we have synthesized their issues, changed names and other details, and dramatized the action so the lessons are clear and applicable across many fields of endeavor. Four chapters describe our framework for creating change by applying the ethnographic approach, by analyzing the case narratives and bringing in other cases and examples.

Chapter 1, A Case of Conflicting Authority, tells the story of "University Hospital," a health care provider that faces an un-ignorable moment when long-standing agreements about how work gets done in the operating room come into conflict with newer agreements that are part of a change initiative to improve patient safety.

Chapter 2, The Un-ignorable Moment, describes those potent cultural moments (such as our experience at Bee Lor's funeral) that contain a huge quantity of information and potential for catalyzing change. Every company that tries to transform or reinvent itself in some way comes up against such moments, and must learn how to understand them and unleash the positive energy that is contained within them.

Chapter 3, A Case of Adaptive Identity, explores the challenges facing Quire, a global software company that has grown through acquisition and has built up considerable debt. To avoid becoming an acquisition target itself, the company has to make a strategic transition from cost-cutting and efficiency to double-digit organic growth within three years.

Chapter 4, Finding the Future Inside, describes how to locate the elements of your culture that you can build on for future success. We call these "found pilots"—people, places, and projects where the desired cultural practices are already happening. By harnessing the success of these found pilots, you can make a smoother transition from old to new.

Chapter 5, Sweeping People In, looks at how you can mobilize people's energy in service of the new cultural agreements your company needs to fulfill its strategic commitments—especially in organizations that are complex and resistant to change. The ability to mobilize people's energy is enhanced when you use social networking tools to engage those who may not agree with you.

Chapter 6, The Case of the Leader Who Finds a New Kind of Power, relates the difficulties of the newly appointed president of Moncrieff University, who devises a brilliant plan to bring the institution out of its financial troubles and into the international spotlight. Unfortunately, he fails to engage important leaders on and off campus and finds himself facing a powerful wave of resistance from the faculty and the board of trustees.

Chapter 7, Leading Leaders, describes the challenges of leading when your followers are, in effect, volunteers—people who manage their own careers and have multiple affiliations. Leaders can no longer "command and control" but must learn to "command and collaborate." Leaders can no longer push for results but must create pull for achieving them by mobilizing the passion, interests, and energy of others.

ONE FINAL THOUGHT BEFORE YOU READ FURTHER. As you begin to tap into your culture to enable change, you'll find others within the organization right there with you. But there will be some who show little interest in participating in the new cultural agreements. You may find yourself thinking that such people are acting in a resistant, inauthentic, or artificial way. When that happens, remember the "native's point of view." Behavior is culturally prescribed. Those resisters are likely acting in ways that are culturally considered to be the normal and natural way to do things. Having at your disposal a variety of ways to form cultural agreements provides you with the flexibility you need to create change in turbulent times.

As it turns out, there are many ways to attend a funeral.[7]

CHAPTER 1

A Case of
Conflicting Authority

W HEN I ARRIVED AT University Hospital at 7:52 AM that wintry morning, everything looked normal. Nothing about the place suggested that it was on the brink of becoming dysfunctional, as Andrea Crowley had remarked when she called me the night before. But then organizations that are coming apart at the seams don't necessarily show it. *And what organizations aren't coming apart at the seams these days,* I thought.

Andrea Crowley was the chief nursing officer at UH, the person responsible for the nursing staff and nursing support personnel, as well as their training and performance. She had called me just after 11:00 PM the evening before to say there had been an "incident" at the hospital just two days earlier. Now it had escalated into a "situation." She had been charged with managing the issue. She didn't have time to look for a consultant and wasn't even sure UH needed one, or if so, what kind, but was sure she needed help. Our firm—a small consultancy that focuses on strategic, organizational, and cultural issues—had worked successfully with University Hospital on several assignments over the years, so Crowley's boss thought of us. Crowley, however, was new in her position and we had never met. She sounded concerned on the phone. I agreed to come in and talk.

As I drove in that morning, the word "incident" kept running through my mind. Interesting. What kind of incident was she talking about? What might be going on at UH that required such immediate attention that an experienced executive would call in a consultant she didn't know? Clearly it was not a minor operational issue or an organizational design problem. An incident sounded like a word used in international diplomacy. *The incident involved an unidentified aircraft flying over restricted airspace.*

What could it possibly be? How could a single incident escalate in two days to push an organization to the brink of dysfunction? I didn't know the details, but I had an idea about the nature of the incident—one of those troubling but ultimately revealing events that we call an "un-ignorable moment." And, as it turned out, I was right.

Andrea Crowley met me at the elevator on the tenth floor, led me into her office, and closed the door firmly behind us. "Thank you for coming in, Mr. O'Connor," she said. We sat at a small conference table next to a window overlooking the hospital atrium where wheelchairs and gurneys and white coats moved about.

After asking Andrea to please call me Mal, I asked, "What happened?"

Crowley took a deep breath. "Tuesday morning, a patient came in to the ER in distress. Severe diverticulitis. Suspected rupture of the large intestine. Risk of abdominal infection. Miraculously, one of our best surgeons was available. Surgery was tougher than expected. There were complications. Near the end, there was a sudden increase in bleeding. The surgery lasted eight hours."

"The team must have been pretty beat."

Crowley nodded. "As the surgeon was preparing to close up, the scrub tech conducted the post-op count."

"That's mandatory, of course."

"Yes, to ensure all instruments and sponges are accounted for."

"A forgotten sponge can prove fatal, I know."

"And provoke a lawsuit."

"Yes. Something went wrong?"

"The scrub tech came up one sponge short."

"Not unusual."

"Not at all. That's why we do the count. The scrub tech informed the surgeon. But the surgeon ignored the information and started to close up the incision."

"I see."

"As I understand it, the scrub tech spoke up again, more forcefully. Still the doctor ignored the scrub. This is where it

gets confusing. There were strong words. The scrub tech somehow came between the patient and the doctor. He may have
reached for, even grabbed, the stapler. Somehow it came out
of the doctor's hands. The surgeon stumbled toward the patient. Maybe fell across him. Maybe it was the scrub tech who
shielded the patient with his own body. Anyway, for a moment,
things were seriously out of control."

"Wow." This was all very odd.

"Fortunately," Crowley continued, "the nurse was able to
get the situation under control. I don't quite know how or what
she did. But the missing sponge was located. The incision was
closed. The operation was completed successfully." Crowley
looked at me very deliberately. "I want to stress that the patient's safety was never in jeopardy."

"I understand." We paused for a moment. It was certainly
not unusual for a sponge to go missing. But for a scrub tech to
challenge a surgeon? And for there to be some kind of physical
interaction, if not altercation, in an operating room—that indeed
amounted to an incident. However, Crowley hadn't been there.
It had been a long surgery. Everyone was tired. Who knows
what "really" happened.

"What does the scrub tech say about it?" I asked.

"I haven't talked with him. Yet. I suppose I should." The
prospect did not seem to appeal to her very much.

"What about the surgeon?"

"I haven't talked with him either. There's been no time.
And . . ." She didn't say it, but I had the sense that she wasn't
sure what she should do.

"Who have you talked with?"

"Only the nurse's supervisor."

"But nobody who was actually in the room?"

"No. I wasn't sure what I should do. I thought it might just blow over. After all, the patient is fine. Nobody was hurt. There seemed to be no lasting effects."

We sat in silence for a moment. Why, I wondered, would a surgeon choose to ignore the scrub tech's information? What would cause a scrub tech to be so assertive? Why would harsh words be necessary, if indeed they were used? What was really going on between these two? It was an incident, for sure. And such moments often are manifestations of some deeper issue.

"How are things going generally at the hospital?" I asked.

"I've only been here a year. There's been a lot of . . . turmoil."

"Of what kind?"

"About six months ago, we started a new initiative to improve patient safety. It's called Putting Patients First. Zero preventable errors. That's our goal."

"How's it going?"

"It's been difficult. Many people don't like it. Some have refused to participate. Some actively badmouth the approach."

"Sounds like the incident in the OR might be connected to this initiative?"

"Well, possibly. The surgeon is not a fan of Putting Patients First."

"I see." I thought for a moment. "You said that the incident has escalated and it's now a situation. What do you mean by that?"

Crowley sighed. "Everyone's on edge. Dr. Piersen has demanded the scrub tech be fired. Other OR personnel are refusing to work with Piersen. We've had to postpone some nonessential surgeries. In-patients are hearing all kinds of rumors and some are getting nervous. Prospective patients are asking lots of questions before they commit to us. Even the board of trustees has gotten wind of the incident and they are expecting a report from our CEO."

She shrugged and attempted a smile. "I need help. It feels like the place is flying apart. My assignment is to find out what happened and make some recommendations about what to do next. But I have no idea what really happened. And I'm certainly not sure what we should do next. That's why I called you."

"Okay. I'll do my best to help. The first thing to do is talk with the people who were directly involved. Starting with the surgeon."

Crowley twitched. "You want to talk with Dr. Piersen?"

"Yes, I do."

"Okay," she said. "I'll set it up." She reached for the phone and looked at me with what I read as sympathy. "This should be interesting."

———

WITH THAT FIRST, BRIEF CONVERSATION, I had begun a process at University Hospital that we call "listening in." Barry and I had learned about listening in during our early days as ethnographers, working in various cultural communities. I would sit and listen, observing, taking notes, occasionally asking a question as people went about their daily lives—as Barry and I had done with the Hmong community in Philadelphia. At University Hospital, I would not have that much time, but I did have the advantage of experience since I had been in situations like this before with other hospital clients.

Listening in involves deliberately taking a pause, listening to individuals and groups about what's going on—often as they go about their daily lives—asking questions, and recognizing signals when your own assumptions are getting in the way. After hearing a great deal, thinking about causes, and talking about courses of action, you are ready to explain how you have incorporated what you've heard from people into your strategies and initiatives.

Far too few people spend time listening in, especially when they're under tremendous pressure, and instead take hasty action that throws the company into an even messier state than the one they tried to fix. Listening in takes practice but pays off. Slowing down helps you to speed up.

But slowing down to listen in is hard when things are coming apart at the seams, as they seemed to be at UH.

———————

THE DAY AFTER MY MEETING with Andrea Crowley, I was slotted into Dr. Piersen's schedule for a twenty-three-minute interview. Not thirty minutes or an hour. Not a fifteen-minute call. *Twenty-three minutes.* As I was walking from the parking garage to the main entrance of the hospital, I got a call from the chief medical officer at University Hospital, Dr. Darren Davidian. He was the man responsible for the medical staff and procedures at the institution. A big job. He was the one who had asked Andrea Crowley to find out what was going on, and also the one who had recommended that she call us. We had worked together, tangentially, on a couple of earlier projects. He was no doubt taking heat from people above, below, and all around him.

"Mr. O'Connor," he said. "Thanks for jumping on this issue so quickly."

"Of course."

"I just wanted to catch you before your conversation with Leonard. Dr. Piersen. I expect you're headed there now?"

"That's right. I'm glad you called. The more information I have the better."

"Well, as you undoubtedly know, Dr. Piersen is an incredibly important player here. He's our chief of gastroenterology. President of the medical staff. I'm sure you know of him, if you don't know him directly."

Oh yes. Everybody knew of Piersen. A major name in the medical community. Involved in politics, philanthropy, and the arts, both in the metro region and on the national level.

"Leonard runs the most successful group practice in the city, possibly the region. He attracts patients to UH from all over the world. Residents kill, as it were, to work with him. He's our rock star. Our franchise player."

"I understand."

"All of that is not to say, however, that Leonard is a perfect guy. He is what you might expect of a top-ranked, incredibly busy surgeon. He does not suffer fools gladly. He worships precision. He can be prickly. But he is a top surgeon and a thoroughgoing professional."

"I understand. I have twenty-three minutes scheduled with him."

Davidian chuckled. "Is there anything further you need to know before you talk with him?"

"Yes. What can you tell me about the status of your new patient safety program? Putting Patients First. Zero preventable errors."

"It's largely about following protocols and procedures."

"The sponge count being one of them."

"Yes, that one isn't particularly new or controversial. But we have introduced many of them, some mandated by various professional and governmental oversight bodies, some we have developed ourselves. In addition to these very specific and detailed protocols, there is a set of recommended practices for professional conduct, team behavior, that extend into every area of activity. Operating room. Clinical and nonclinical activities. It's quite extensive and we're proud to be leading the way in this regard."

"I see. And what connection do you identify between the initiative and what happened in the operating room the other day?"

"That's easy. One of the key tenets of Putting Patients First is that *everybody* in the hospital has a responsibility for patient

safety. Everybody, whatever their role or function, has a responsibility to speak up about any issue in that regard. *If you see
something, say something.* That's the mantra."

"What was the impetus for the program? Do you have a
patient safety issue?"

"Absolutely not."

"I assume you have data to support that."

"Of course we do. Just let me know what you need."

My phone buzzed—time for my appointment with Dr.
Piersen. "I'll be in touch," I said.

DR. LEONARD PIERSEN was not as imperious as I had been expecting. He was gracious and charming, greeting me with a
warm handshake and even a light pat on the shoulder. He was
lean and fit, in his early sixties, with silver-white hair and slim,
strong surgeon's hands. We sat across from each other in leather
chairs around a low, round table with nothing on it except a
small carved figure of a downhill skier.

Piersen wasted no time. "You are some kind of consultant, I'm
told. And you are investigating the case of the missing sponge."

"Yes. I'm just trying to understand what happened in the
OR that day."

"Of course you are." Dr. Piersen leaned forward. "The surgery was complex. Acute diverticulitis. The patient came close
to bleeding out. I'm told you have a PhD in folklore. You may
understand what it's like to be responsible for bringing a person

back from the dead." He looked at me with a faint smile. "Isn't that what shamans do?"

"Shamans operate in high-risk environments. They have a lot of responsibility. They have to earn the trust of their patients. Of course, there is a critical difference between shamans and surgeons."

Piersen raised an eyebrow. "Which is?"

"No one questions a shaman's authority."

Piersen looked at me deadpan, then returned to the story. "As I was getting ready to set the first staple, the scrub tech yelled at me. I have never worked with this guy before. He has a rather distinct accent, so I couldn't understand exactly what he said, but it was something about sponges. I knew there were no sponges in the patient."

"You counted them?"

"Yes. I have performed hundreds of surgeries. Never once have I left anything inside a patient that wasn't supposed to be there."

"I see."

"But that's not the point. The proper procedure is for the nurse to do the sponge count, not the scrub tech. This nurse, Sheri McGlynn, has been with me in countless surgeries. I trust her completely. I can't be talking to every scrub tech in the middle of surgery. It's distracting. Indeed it's dangerous."

"I see."

"There's a clear chain of command in the operating room for one very good reason. *Patient safety*. That's the only way to ensure the best outcome for the patient."

"But, as I understand it, there *was* a missing sponge."

Piersen looked sharply at me. "It wasn't missing."

"What do you mean?"

Piersen spoke almost off-handedly. "The scrub tech put it there."

"Wait a minute. You're saying that the scrub tech deliberately put a sponge inside the patient?"

"Yes, when he yelled at me the second time he threw himself across the operating table and tried to grab the stapler. I lost a bit of balance. Stepped back. Turned away for a second. Sheri was attending to me. It was a perfect opportunity. The scrub tech could easily have popped in a sponge."

"Why would he do that?"

"To be a hero, of course. I'm sure you've learned about this program called Putting Patients First. Zero preventable errors."

"Surely the program does not encourage people to plant sponges in patients."

"No, but the program does offer incentives and rewards and recognition for those who supposedly advance the cause. This guy might have benefited or at least thought he could benefit. He may also have just been trying to keep his job. In addition to the safety program, we're also in the middle of a cost-cutting initiative. Head count reduction. I don't know what was going on inside that guy's head."

"The Putting Patients First program involves a number of new protocols and standard operating room routines, as I understand it."

"Yes, soon the surgeon will be like the airline pilot. With no authority to do anything that does not adhere to some guideline dreamed up by a government bureaucrat or an insurance company underwriter who has never been inside an operating theater. That, I assure you, will not improve the quality of patient care in this hospital. Or this country."

He smiled. "What else can I tell you?"

Not much, as it turned out. Due to a scheduling issue, Piersen's time for me had been cut from twenty-three minutes to thirteen. The listening in was out, at least as far as Dr. Piersen was concerned.

———————————

OVER THE NEXT SEVERAL DAYS, I did a good deal more "listening in" elsewhere at the hospital. I talked with several senior people as well as nurses and midlevel staffers. I also spent a fair amount of time just hanging out, listening in on lunch conversations and hallway talk, chatting with anyone I could connect with. It didn't take long for people to learn that I was "some kind of consultant" trying to learn what was going on. As a result, some people gave me a wide berth. Others wanted to tell me everything.

What did I learn through the listening in? That the sponge incident was not an anomaly at University Hospital. It was only the latest, most disruptive, most visible, and most worrisome of many such conflicts, large and small, that had erupted throughout the hospital in the past several months, coinciding exactly with the introduction of the Putting Patients First program.

I also came to understand that the program itself was a manifestation of pressure the hospital was feeling from outside forces. There was the surgical safety checklist, which had recently been issued by the World Health Organization (WHO). And the Medicare Quality Reporting program, which mandated use of the checklist as part of regular hospital routine. There was a good reason for the mandate. Research reported in the *New England Journal of Medicine* showed that using the checklist could reduce surgical complications by a third and mortality by half. There were the pressures of the Affordable Care Act. And demands from the chair of the UH board of trustees that UH become known *worldwide* as a leader in patient safety.

I also pieced together that Piersen had been under an inordinate amount of personal stress lately. One of the partners in his practice had died suddenly, meaning that more surgeries—as well as management of the group practice—fell to Piersen. He had taken on the role of head of the medical staff at the hospital, essentially the spokesperson for all the doctors in the system. What's more, Dr. Piersen was one of the longest-serving doctors performing surgeries at UH, and his tenure predated that of Dr. Davidian, Andrea Crowley, and the CEO. In other words, he knew where more bodies were buried (literally and figuratively) than anybody else in the system.

All of that put the organization structure under tremendous stress. And the UH culture, which determined the way things get done, was being forced into new ways of working that it did not fully understand or accept. Inevitably, there would be more incidents and more stress. And sometimes, in hindsight, you can look back and say, *that was the moment when it all started coming apart.*

———

MY CONVERSATION WITH THE SCRUB TECH, Marco Fierro, added a whole new layer of meaning.

I met Fierro in the hospital cafeteria, which was clearly making an effort to provide healthy, locally sourced food, lots of greens and soups and dishes prepared to appeal to the various ethnic populations that made the hospital run—Southeast Asian, Somali, Eastern European, Hispanic—as well as standard American fare.

"I've been on duty ten hours already," Fierro said when he finally showed up, ten minutes late.

"In the OR?"

"No. I'm banned from the operating room until this gets figured out."

"But you're still working ten hours a day? Is that typical?"

"Oh yeah. The shifts change all the time. I never know exactly when I will work or how long. Six hours. Ten hours. Twelve hours. It doesn't help with the family life, you know."

As Piersen had said, Marco did have an accent—I guessed Peruvian—but it was not so "distinct" that it would make the word "sponge" unintelligible.

"What happened that day in the OR?" I asked.

"Let me ask you something first," Fierro said. "You're here to figure out whether I should be fired. Is that right?"

"No. I've been asked to try to find out exactly what happened."

"That's not the word on the street. When consultants come around, the next thing you know people get fired."

"I know. But I have no authority to fire anybody."

"You can recommend it."

"Listen. I'm here to listen to you. I want to hear all sides of the story."

"Really?" He looked at me closely. "That's funny because you are the first person to ask. Don't you think that's a little strange?"

I did think it was strange, if not unusual, but I didn't say so. I shrugged.

Fierro shrugged in return. "I don't know. I guess it's better to tell my story than to let somebody else make it up."

"Maybe you could start just by telling me about your job. What exactly do you do? What's your role in the operating room?"

Marco seemed flattered by my interest. "My job in the OR," he said with pride, "is to maintain the highest possible sterile standards. During every surgical procedure. Instruments. Equipment. Gowns. Gloves. Do you know how much stuff we go through in an eight-hour operation like the one we're talking about? I have to be constantly on the lookout."

"So you have a direct impact on patient safety."

"Of course I do. I'm the infection fighter, man. Always have been. But now even more than ever."

"Why is that?"

"Putting Patients First!" He smiled slightly. "It gives me just a tiny little bit of power. It gives me a little authority. A voice, you know? Do you know how many times I have seen a surgeon do something I think is wrong? But what could I do? I could never speak to the surgeon. I couldn't call him out. He would probably fire me on the spot."

"But now . . ."

"*See something, say something.* You've seen the signs around. With this new program, that's what I'm supposed to do. And that's what I did. I saw something. That we had lost a sponge. Could easily be inside. I said something. What's the big deal? That's what they told us to do."

"Did you have any physical contact with Dr. Piersen?"

"I didn't think he heard me. Or didn't understand me. He's always asking me to repeat myself. He says it's because of my accent. I say he's a little bit hard of hearing. So I reached over the operating table. I touched his hand to get his attention."

"Then what happened?"

"He freaked out."

"He dropped the stapler, right?"

Marco looked at me as if I were crazy. "*Dropped* the stapler? The guy *threw* the stapler at me. If you don't believe me, go look at the wall. There's a dent where the damn thing hit."

I took a moment to let this sink in.

Marco leaned forward. "I have never done anything like this before. I have nothing against Dr. Piersen. I don't even care if he threw a stapler at me. Big deal. I just don't get why everybody is going crazy because I did just what they told me to do."

He shook his head. "I can tell you that plenty of people around here are wondering what's going on. Not about what happened in the OR. But what '*see something, say something*' really means. Maybe they got the words wrong. Maybe that second 'something' should have been a 'nothing.'"

THEN THERE WAS THE QUESTION of the data that Dr. Davidian had delivered via his information technology group.

I had one of our analysts, Ravi, check out the patient safety data at University Hospital. Not long after my talk with Marco, I got a call from him.

"I have an interesting finding," he said. "The hospital has an almost perfect patient safety record. Ninety-six percent. Almost no errors."

"Really?" I had done enough work with health care institutions to know that no hospital has that kind of record across the board. "That's not possible."

"There's nothing wrong with the data." Ravi chuckled. "So far as it goes."

"Meaning?"

"This Putting Patients First initiative, in addition to all the protocols and practices, also involves a big push to gather a ton more data about errors and mistakes than ever before."

"So the data they gave you were gathered through the Putting Patients First program?"

"Yes. That's right."

"And it shows they have a perfect record?"

"Precisely. No problems. No adverse outcomes. Not a bedsore or a dropped bedpan, no patient falls, no bloodstream infections. Not a sponge gone astray."

"But it only goes back six months."

"Well, that's one issue, but there is plenty of earlier info, even though it's all over the map. But the main problem is that the new data comes from only 40 percent of the departments that are supposed to report. And the ones that did report are the ones that are the least relevant to patient safety."

"You're saying that 60 percent of the hospital is not complying with the request for safety data as part of this Putting Patients First program?"

"Right. And only one surgical group reported."

"So maybe their record is not as good as they think it is." Could they be living with one of those self-perpetuating institutional beliefs? *We're great at patient safety because we think we are.*

"Well, the one group that reported did, in fact, have a perfect record."

"Do you know which group it is?"

"Green. Marshall. Doctor."

DR. MARSHALL GREEN. How could his group have a perfect patient safety record? Was the data for real? Perhaps this was the next place to explore. Not because Dr. Green had been involved in the sponge incident, but to find out why he hadn't been. Perhaps this was a place at University Hospital where the future already lived, where the idea of Putting Patients First was already a reality. Where new ways of working and new agreements had already taken hold.

I called Dr. Green's office expecting to find myself trapped in an endless telephonic maze. Green himself picked up.

"Hi. Can I help you?" Indeed, he had a helpful tone. I introduced myself. Dr. Green knew all about me. I asked about the data.

"Yes, we're proud of the safety record in our unit," Green said. "No errors over a three-year period."

"Three years? I thought the data was only for the past six months."

"That's only the data we collected specifically in the Putting Patients First format. But our surgical unit has been tracking performance for much longer than that. We operate a little differently than the other units in the hospital."

"How so?"

"Nothing special, really. We work with a team-based model. Interdisciplinary teams of physicians, nurses, and others. PAs, pharmacists, social workers. All the team members interact with the patients and their families."

Hmm. Quite different from Piersen's command-and-control approach. Dr. Green explained how each person in his unit had a clear understanding of his or her role and how all were encouraged to practice to the full extent of their licensure and training. This made it possible for the lowest-cost person to do much more than was typical throughout the hospital—within the range of his or her profession, of course.

"The team-based approach helps us deliver the highest quality care and also keep costs down," Green told me. "And I think we provide a pretty exceptional patient experience, too."

"Do you believe there's a correlation between the way you're organized and your performance on patient safety?"

"Absolutely no question."

"Have any other groups in the hospital adopted your approach?"

Dr. Green chuckled. "No, but it's not for lack of trying. Listen, I've been going on about continuous practice improvement and the team-based approach to patient care for years. I've talked to most of the other surgeons about it, but they all have their own ways. I didn't get any traction until Andrea Crowley came on board. The eyes of the new, you know."

"The Putting Patients First program was modeled on your approach?"

"With some modifications and additions."

"How do you think it's doing?"

Dr. Green snorted. "It's limping. The initiative was rushed. The introduction wasn't well executed. It kind of got rammed down everybody's throat. We had a one-day meeting and that was that. No setup and not much follow-through. It was hard to tell what the goal was. The whole thing got reduced to checklists and protocols, because compliance with the World Health Organization guidelines is the most pressing issue. But without the context of teamwork and a new definition of roles and behaviors needed, they can be more of a bother than a help. But everybody is expected to use the mechanisms and gather data on performance."

"Was there any training or further support?"

"Spotty. Department heads were responsible for training their own people. They didn't have the time or skills. Who knows what people were taught, or what they learned from that. I suspect that many people had no training at all."

"Could that be why so few units have reported their safety data?"

"Absolutely. It was not at all clear what was required. There was no kind of consequence if you didn't report."

"Was Dr. Piersen's team working with the new protocols and checklists on the day of the incident?"

"Most likely."

"What do you make of the incident?"

Green paused. "I really don't know. But if anybody knows, it's Sheri McGlynn."

I DON'T THINK SHERI MCGLYNN RELISHED the idea of being listened in on. Not everybody welcomes being interrogated by a person who is fascinated by your job and makes frequent references to folk cultures.

Finally she agreed to meet at a coffee shop a couple of blocks from the hospital. I had been picturing Sheri as the savior in the situation: the level-headed nurse who had managed to prevent a potentially explosive situation from actually exploding. That was not the impression I had of her when she finally darted in, fourteen minutes late. She looked stressed, pinched. I had taken a liking to Dr. Piersen's way with timekeeping.

"I need to get back soon," she said, as she slid onto the seat across from me.

"Okay," I said. "But Dr. Green thinks very highly of you and suggested we talk. You were obviously right in the middle of things."

"The nurse is always in the middle," she snapped. There was resignation and frustration in her tone. "Now more than ever."

Sheri looked out the window at passersby. I thought for a moment she might get up and leave. Finally, she turned a penetrating gaze on me. "The hospital has become an almost impossible place to work. I have been there for nearly eighteen years and it's never been like this."

I had not expected this. "How?'

"I just don't know what's what anymore. I have worked incredibly hard to develop a good relationship with Dr. Piersen. That hasn't been easy. It took time. But we work well together. Or we did, anyway, until all this new stuff."

"The Putting Patients First program?"

"Yes. That. The protocols and checklists. The reporting. The attitude. Andrea Crowley comes down on me if we don't comply. Dr. Piersen comes down on me if we do or try to. I used to be the one who had authority for the scrub techs and other support staff in the OR. Now it's like people can do whatever they want. If Marco thinks he should challenge a doctor, what am I supposed to do? Whose side am I on? Why are there sides at all?"

"That sounds difficult."

"Plus, we have all the new requirements for data reporting, but they don't tell us what it's going to be used for. Are they just trying to check up on the surgeons? It's like I'm being asked to spy on my colleagues. I can't do that. If we do have an error, then what?"

I waited. She calmed down a little.

"So, what happened in the OR that day?"

Sheri looked at me hard, as if trying to make a decision.

"Nothing happened. We had a tough surgery. Everybody did their job. The patient came through and is now recovering at home. Nothing out of the ordinary happened."

"There was no disagreement? Dr. Piersen and the scrub tech had some kind of . . ."

Sheri looked at me coldly. "Kind of what? What did you hear?"

"Well . . ." Was she saying there had *not* been a problem? She obviously knew what the rumors were and why I was ranging around the place.

"Mr. O'Connor," she said. "Lots of things happen in operating rooms that might look strange to outsiders. I don't know what you've been told or by who. But it's not my job to evaluate the actions of a surgeon. Especially to someone outside the hospital. Nor is it my job anymore, as far as I can tell, to supervise the scrub techs. I just have to keep my head down and my mind on my own tasks. And that's what I plan to do from now on."

She gathered herself. I had been hoping for the "real" story about the incident in the operating room, but I had gotten something more valuable: a personal perspective that made it clearer than ever that this was about larger issues, not an individual incident.

Sheri hesitated a moment, as if unsure whether to proceed. "I could tell you one thing, though."

I sensed this was important. I said nothing.

She leaned toward me and lowered her voice. "Dr. Piersen does *not* have as good a patient safety record as you might assume. Or as some people think."

I had no idea where she was headed but did not want her to stop. "Oh."

She now seemed committed to her revelation. "It's true he has never left anything inside a patient. As far as I know. But he's had other problems. *Chronically.*"

"And is this . . . known?"

Sheri scoffed. "Of course it's known. Everybody knows. Everyone's afraid to challenge him on it. No one can figure out why we don't follow Dr. Green's model. You know that his group has an almost perfect safety performance."

Could I trust the nurse's information? Did she have enough knowledge to make this claim or was she just going on her own observations?

"You're wondering how I know this," she said.

"Yes."

"There's a report," she said.

"About Piersen's patient safety record?"

"Yes. It was done before Andrea Crowley came on board. She doesn't even know about it."

"Is it available? Where can I find it?"

Sheri glanced around the coffee shop, reached into her bag, pulled out a thin folder, and slid it across the table to me.

I looked at the cover. "Patient Safety at University Hospital, by Dr. Leonard Piersen." He had written it himself? When I looked up, I saw Sheri hurrying along the sidewalk outside my window. She did not look back at me.

"SO, MR. O'CONNOR, what do you have to tell us?" Dr. Davidian asked.

It was a Friday morning and we were all gathered in the office of the chief medical officer, the penthouse suite on the twenty-first floor of University Hospital. It had been about ten days since the Incident of the Missing Sponge, and now it was time for me to present my thoughts to Davidian, Crowley, and Piersen. The office was huge, with windows on three sides, overlooking the city. A good spot for a 40,000-foot overview, if not a particularly good place for listening in to what's happening in the hospital.

"So, what have you got?" Davidian asked. "A total solution, I hope!" An attempt at jocularity.

"No, I don't have a total solution," I said. "But I think I can define the problem." I paused.

"That's a start, I guess," said Davidian, with just an edge of irritability. "What is it?"

"Let me start with what it's not."

Piersen made a small mouth noise and glanced at his watch. "I have a surgery in fifty-two minutes."

"It's not an issue about an interpersonal conflict," I said. "It's not about Dr. Piersen's behavior in the operating room. Or about what Marco Fierro did or did not do."

"Who is Marco Fierro?" Piersen asked.

"The scrub tech." Crowley looked at Dr. Piersen with mild disbelief. *He doesn't even know the guy's name?*

"Okay," said Davidian. "So if you don't consider this to be a matter of personal performance or misperformance, then you don't see the need for a review or censure or anything of that sort?"

"Probably not."

"It's a matter of protocols?" Crowley asked. "Or operating room procedure?"

Piersen rolled his eyes. "Spare us more checklists, Mr. O'Connor, please."

"No," I said. "I'm not an expert on OR procedure by any means, but the protocols aren't the main source of the problem."

I paused again. Looks of consternation.

"The problem is bigger than either a personnel conflict or a procedural shortcoming."

No one really wanted me to continue. It would be so simple to chastise a lowly scrub tech. Or to discreetly caution Dr. Piersen. Or to add another mechanism. Or restructure something. Or make a new rule. Give someone the task. Make sure they did it. Problem solved.

Crowley cleared her throat. As a newcomer, she probably

was in the weakest position, but she also was less invested in the old ways. "It's about patient safety, isn't it?"

I looked at Dr. Piersen. "Indirectly, yes," I said. Piersen noticeably straightened and then pressed two fingers together until they turned white.

"We have an excellent patient safety record here at University Hospital," Davidian said just a bit too forcefully.

"Yes, I know you believe that," I said. "Although the data might not fully support the claim."

"What do you mean?" Davidian was now genuinely upset and looked quite ready to kill the messenger. "Our latest data put us at 96 percent error-free performance. That's way above the national average."

"Yes," I said. "But as I understand it, the survey had only a 40 percent response rate."

"What?" Davidian looked genuinely surprised.

"Yes. And only one of your [seven] surgical units responded." I considered mentioning the high response rate from the kitchen and maintenance units, but decided against it.

I glanced at Piersen. "I know that some surgical units have been tracking their own data over time, although they have not shared it hospital-wide. Some of that data tells a different story."

"Oh really?" Davidian sensed that I knew more.

"Yes," I said. "The data I've seen suggest there have been significantly more errors than are being reported. Thankfully none of them has resulted in a serious breach of patient safety. Although they could have."

I let this sink in.

Davidian gathered his thoughts. "So our problem is one of survey methodology, perhaps, or compliance? Is that what you're saying?"

"No, I think it's even more significant and fundamental than that."

I had their full attention now, but sensed I was on the brink of exasperating them with my indirect approach.

"We've probably had enough of what the problem is not," Davidian said. "Could we please move along to what you think it is?"

"Of course," I said. "The problem is right here in this room."

I noticed Piersen's left eye twitch. "What do you mean?" he asked.

"It's quite simple," I said. "You have a problem of conflicting authority."

Everyone stiffened. Were they not the authorities in the hospital?

"No one in this hospital is completely sure who has responsibility for patient safety," I said. "Who has it? When do they have it? Why do they have it?"

Silence. I could hear them thinking. *Is this right?*

Dr. Piersen finally spoke up. "The surgeon has the final authority in the operating room. Full stop."

"Certainly when it comes to the surgical process itself," I said. "But is the surgeon the final authority in every interaction within the operating room? In prepping the OR? In how a nurse comforts a patient? In counting sponges? Authority is situational, relational, temporal."

I paused.

Davidian spoke next. "I'm the chief medical officer. I have authority for overall patient care at this hospital. The buck stops with me."

"Yes, but you answer to a host of regulatory bodies and insurance companies. Their requirements change constantly. You have to synthesize all of that into a set of hospital practices."

"And damned frustrating it is, too," Davidian admitted.

"Plus, you don't really have authority over the doctors who have to carry out the practices."

"Yes, of course I do," he blurted out. He thought for a moment, glanced at Piersen, then retreated slightly. "Nominally, anyway."

"Nominally," repeated Piersen, with a flicker of amusement. He had relaxed a little now that he knew I wasn't going to call him out on his secret data.

"I have authority over the nursing and support staff," said Crowley.

"Sure you do," I agreed, "when it comes to hiring and performance evaluation. But the Putting Patients First initiative blurs the lines of authority. Marco thought that the 'see something, say something' imperative gave him the power to act as he did, in the furtherance of patient safety."

"Yes, but I also have responsibility for training," Crowley said. "So if Marco didn't completely understand the initiative, that's still my responsibility." She seemed ready to shoulder all blame for the authority issue.

"Maybe. You became the champion for patient safety improvement, but you didn't really have the resources to implement the program fully. Nor were you able to get the full support of the medical staff. As a result, the more complex aspects of the Putting Patients First approach, particularly team-based surgery, were pushed aside and the program ended up looking like a checklist."

"I'm fine with the damned checklist," Piersen barked. "We've worked with checklists and all that nonsense for years. And my unit has an excellent patient safety record."

"Ah," I said. I paused. I hoped that Davidian would see an opening.

"So it was your unit that reported in through Putting Patients First?" Davidian asked.

Piersen, for all his sharpness and bluster and time obsession, was a highly principled person. He was not going to deceive. "No, we haven't reported. Yet. But we have been tracking performance. I have never been sued for an error. Never lost a patient because of an error. Never cut the wrong piece off anybody."

Silence. It was Crowley who probed a little deeper. Perhaps she did know about the secret report.

"So you tracked lawsuits, mortality, and wrong-site surgery?"

"Yes," Piersen replied.

"Anything else?" she asked. "Like readmissions?"

Piersen looked out the window for what seemed like a long time. "Well, yes, okay. We have had some issues with readmissions. And infections." He turned back to the group. "But they're relatively minor and I've been working with Sheri McGlynn to improve things."

I thought Piersen had taken enough heat for the moment. "Which brings us to her, the nurse," I said. "She has an authority issue, too. Is she the patient safety watchdog? Does she have the responsibility to stop a procedure when she sees an issue?"

I paused. Davidian cleared his throat. We spent another twenty-six minutes talking about the issue of authority before the participants had to rush off to other meetings and phone calls and surgeries.

"Well," Davidian said. "We need some time to digest all of this."

"In a way, you were given a gift," I said.

Dr. Piersen, back to his old form, sniffed. "A gift?"

"You had an un-ignorable moment. A clear announcement that the hospital is undergoing a period of exceptional stress. It uncovered a fundamental issue. And, although it has been difficult, nothing fundamentally damaging has happened."

"Well, Mr. O'Connor," Piersen said, "I think you have surfaced an important truth."

"I'm glad you think so. What's that?"

"Life was much simpler when there was only one shaman in the room."

CODA: DAVIDIAN AND CROWLEY worked with the CEO of University Hospital to get his authorization to make Putting Patients First priority one. With his backing, they collaborated with Dr. Green and others throughout the organization to create a cultural shift that was long overdue. But the first thing they did was focus on getting all patient care units to report in on a monthly basis. Within six months, 92 percent of all units in the hospital were reporting data, up from 40 percent, with a goal of 100 percent reporting by year end. The number of medical errors began to decline. It's not that everything suddenly turned perfect overnight. This was the beginning of a multiyear effort. In fact, there were three more un-ignorable incidents—moments when authorities clashed or were unclear—but now the hospital staff members were able to recognize them as such and find solutions more quickly than before. Along the way, people in the hospital came to believe that a zero preventable patient injury goal was no longer a dream but a real possibility.

And, oh yes, Dr. Piersen and Dr. Green began to play squash together and eventually joined forces to champion the cause of patient safety throughout the hospital.

Not long after our engagement with University Hospital came to an end, I was browsing in a shop that specializes in folkloric artifacts and came across an intriguing item: a Yoruba shaman's mask. On an impulse, I sent it to Dr. Piersen as a gift.

A few weeks later I received a note of thanks from him, which read: "Africa, here I come."

CHAPTER 2

The Un-ignorable
Moment

YOU COULD INTERPRET THE INCIDENT at University Hospital in a number of different ways. It could be read as a struggle between a powerful surgeon and a frontline technician. Or you could focus on the surgeon's fatigue and overwork, and how this may have clouded his judgment in the moment. These interpretations are not incorrect. By calling this a "moment that can't be ignored," though, we want to highlight how an incident like this goes beyond the interaction of two individuals and calls attention to the clash of two organizational cultures, two systems for getting work done. These are times when culture hits the fan, and the role of individuals and the systems they work in come under tremendous pressure. Un-ignorable moments are ripe with power and information. They demand our attention. When one occurs, there can be no turning back.

These moments typically occur when an organization is teetering on the brink of a cultural shift. It's a time when the collision between an organization's cultures, old and new, produces novel energy and tension, often in a dramatic, uncomfortable way. If handled deftly and with tenacity and sophistication, these moments can illuminate an organization's faults and fissures as it struggles with a changing external environment. In this chapter, we'll explore the nature of these un-ignorable moments, how you know you are facing one, and some ideas for what to do about them.

No two of these moments that can't be ignored look exactly the same, but they share four key characteristics: they are public in nature, they are irreversible, they are systemic, and they challenge the identity of the organization.

IT's PUBLIC

News of the operating room "incident," as it was called at University Hospital, spread like wildfire through the informal communication network. The speed of that communication was one of the reasons the chief nursing officer called us so quickly after it occurred. These moments are public in the sense that they spread throughout the organization or they leak outside to colleagues, partners, investors, or even the general public and media.

Un-ignorable moments may look different in various types of businesses and organizations. In some family businesses, for example, an un-ignorable moment becomes public only within the immediate family and only when members of the next generation discover information about the business their parents had not disclosed. This kind of moment may come up, for example, as a family business faces the challenge of succession from one generation to the next. It is not atypical for a founder or family CEO to keep his or her own counsel on the future, and families often find it difficult to discuss their wishes for the future with each other. Should they keep the business in the family? Are there successors who want to take over? How will liquidity be provided to exiting generations? Sometimes family businesses continue to postpone answering these questions for decades, which can make the un-ignorable moment, when it finally arrives, even more challenging.

This is just what happened to Macleish, Inc., a $700 million family-owned heating and cooling systems business. Henry Macleish, the second-generation leader of the company, was on the verge of selling it to a strategic buyer in the industry. Henry and his wife had three children, all in their thirties. Their son Hank Jr., 38, worked in the business, but Karen, 35, and Robert, 30, had gone into law and teaching, respectively. None of the three had expressed interest in taking over the business or buying Henry out.

Just before the sale was to be effected, Macleish lost two major customers that together accounted for approximately

30 percent of the company's revenue. The buyer got cold feet and tried to change the purchase terms, things reached an impasse, and the deal fell apart.

Henry was frustrated and unsure what to do next. Hank Jr. decided the company needed some outside help. Perhaps the loss of the customers was a wake-up call, an indicator that changes needed to be made. But what should they be? We were asked to work with the family to sort through options.

At our second meeting with the Macleish family, an un-ignorable moment occurred. Henry explained his rationale for selling the business, described why and how the deal had fallen through, and asked his children for their thoughts. What they said was a complete shock to him. In their own ways, Robert, Karen, and Hank Jr. expressed love for the business. They didn't think it should be sold. It should be kept in the family. Henry was dumbfounded. Why hadn't any of them stepped forward earlier? He hadn't wanted to sell the company to an outside buyer at all. In fact, he was disappointed and hurt that none of them had shown any interest in the company. He, too, wanted it to stay in the family. But he was tired and overwhelmed, and didn't think he could carry on anymore.

The three siblings shot right back at Henry. He had never made it clear to them that he wanted the business to stay in the family. He hadn't discussed the possibility of an outside sale with them. Even Hank Jr., who had worked in the family business for ten years, said he wasn't privy to his father's thoughts and was never included in strategic decisions. Karen and Robert agreed they had no say in decisions about governance or plans for the future. They had no idea what would happen if Henry had a stroke or was hit by a bus and couldn't run the company. They didn't even know how many shares they held and what they were worth.

It was quite a moment. What had been tacit—both about what members of the family were thinking and feeling, and about the business and how decisions were made—was now nakedly out on the table. The meeting, which came to be known among family members as the "big shift meeting," marked a genuine turning point for the three siblings in their relationships with each other as well as their relationships with their father. They had to decide whether they wanted to own the business together—not an easy decision because of their different career paths, and also because they assumed it would require a good deal of capital.

Reaching a solution took a few months. In the end, the children proposed a buyout at a price they could manage and with terms acceptable to both father and children. Hank Jr. would run the show. During the process, they realized that their father (and his father before him) had created value beyond the business itself. This was a new perspective for them. They eventually established a family foundation to share some of the family's wealth with the community. And they began to think about how to manage the business for the long term to maximize its benefit for all its stakeholders—including suppliers and customers, the executive team, and themselves.

The Macleish family had a turning-point moment and, because they delved into it and explored it deeply, they enjoyed a highly positive outcome. Sometimes, however, such a moment, as blatant and obvious as it might be, *is* ignored, worsening the problem down the line. This is what happened with Merck's experience with Vioxx, their pain relief drug.

Merck, the global pharmaceutical and chemical company, has long enjoyed a stellar reputation as a research-driven company with strong values and high integrity. The company's leaders were known for putting research before profits and giving scientific development precedence over marketing and cost-cutting.[1] The company felt a deep sense of social responsibility. For example, working with the World Health Organization, it donated its drug Mectizan to fight river blindness in developing countries.[2]

Merck had developed a number of blockbuster drugs over the years—including the asthma drug Singulair, the HPV vaccine Gardasil, and the statin Zocor, which lowers cholesterol. One of the most popular was Vioxx. The medical compound, rofecoxib, was approved for sale by the Food and Drug Administration in May 1999 and went to market as Vioxx. A nonsteroidal anti-inflammatory drug, Vioxx was widely prescribed for arthritis and other acute and chronic pain conditions.[3]

Five years later, it became known that for some patients the use of Vioxx might increase the likelihood of heart problems, strokes, and even death. Merck pulled its medicine off the market in September 2004. Then it came out that Merck had experienced an un-ignorable moment four years earlier and had chosen to look the other way. In May 2000, Merck had learned about the health risks involved with Vioxx but decided to keep marketing the drug while monitoring clinical trials to find out more.[4] Did Merck choose to ignore a moment that, in retrospect, should have been revealing? Or perhaps the company known for values and integrity kept Vioxx on the market simply because it was so lucrative, with worldwide sales of $2.5 billion in the year before it was pulled.[5]

Profit no doubt was a factor, but Merck eventually faced billions of dollars in personal injury lawsuits and a badly tarnished reputation. Why would Merck make such a risky and seemingly uncharacteristic decision? We attribute it to a clash between Merck's existing cultural identity—as the most science-driven of pharmaceutical companies—and newer forces pushing the company to become more commercially focused. Choosing *not* to act on the study that revealed the health risks associated with Vioxx ran counter to the cultural belief system that had guided Merck throughout its long history. Perhaps the decision was so countercultural that Merck could not acknowledge to itself what was happening.[6]

Critical business decisions are always made on the basis of cultural agreements about how work should get done and how decisions should get made. If Merck's decision had proven to be correct, we would now be saying it was sensible. But Merck's identity was too immovable and overconfident to accept challenges to its own cultural beliefs. As Ed Schein,[7] John Kotter,[8] and other experts in organizational culture have pointed out, organizations with the strongest cultures and the greatest success often have the most difficulty changing. Think of the sluggish response the Digital Equipment Corporation (DEC) made to changes in the computer industry in the 1980s.[9] Today, Intel is struggling to find its way in the mobile market after great success with chips for desktop and laptop machines.

Had Merck examined the way its cultural beliefs influenced its decision making, the company's leaders might have recognized the challenge to their scientific credibility as a moment not to be ignored. By 2004, however, the opportunity to make adaptive cultural changes had passed. Vioxx had become a public issue. Although Merck retained its reputation for scientific integrity, its stellar history and reputation were challenged in ways that it absolutely could no longer ignore.

It's Irreversible

These moments are irreversible: they signal that current cultural agreements are now in question, and things will not be going back to business as usual. This is one reason why they must not be ignored!

The US Army offers a good example of how such moments are irreversible. You may think of the Army as stodgy and bureaucratic, but it is one of the most complex and innovative organizations in the world. To put it in perspective, if the US Army were a global corporation, it would have a budget of around $180 billion and would employ more than 1 million people. Culturally speaking, the Army has a history of success in adapting to the challenges of defending the United States, even as those challenges change over time. These challenges go way beyond warfare. They include understanding the location and distribution of natural resources—such as water, food, and minerals—and the effects of their distribution, locally and globally. These in turn have led the Army to produce innovations in the field of knowledge management and organizational learning.

The Army faced an un-ignorable moment during the Vietnam War, when the practice of "fragging" came to light: a soldier using a fragmentation grenade against an officer, either for self-protection or, in some cases, revenge. Many officers were injured and killed in this way. Soldiers favored the fragmentation devices because they were deadly and lacked serial numbers. Consequently, it was impossible to identify the person who threw one.[10]

Although fragging was not unknown before the Vietnam War, the unpopularity of that conflict and the disillusionment associated with it resulted in more incidents. In 1969 the US was pulling out of Vietnam without achieving a victory, but many soldiers remained in combat. The number of fraggings increased, from 96 in 1969 to 209 in 1970, with 34 deaths.[11]

Although Congress began tracking the fragging incidents, the US government said little about them until April 1971, when Democratic senator Mike Mansfield of Montana spoke out. He told the story of a first lieutenant who had lost his life, hit by a grenade intended for another officer. On the floor of the House of Representatives, Republican Charles Mathias of Maryland made note of the moment. Mansfield, he said, had "surfaced" a new term—fragging. "In every war a new vocabulary springs up," Mathias said. "In all the lexicon of war there is not a more tragic word than 'fragging' with all that it implies of total failure of discipline and the depression of morale, the complete sense of frustration and confusion, and the loss of goals and hope itself."[12]

It was an un-ignorable moment that forced the Army to recognize that the perception of the war that fragging had created could not be reversed. It was time to reassess the needs of the military unit to build an environment that would exclude actions like fragging. To help do so, the Army developed a new practice that is now known as the After Action Review (AAR), a three-step process in which an engagement is examined rigorously, openly, and honestly. Business leaders in many industries have adopted a similar practice.

Every member of the AAR team is required to participate in answering three questions:

1. What was supposed to happen?
2. What did happen?
3. What accounts for the difference?[13]

An AAR works best when every team member speaks directly, openly, and honestly regardless of rank or position; but this does not mean that leadership and authority no longer play a role. During an after action review, the leader holds herself and others accountable for actively challenging each participant to speak out, not to place blame but to serve the greater mission. The AAR has become an integral part of training as Army units prepare for duty in Iraq and Afghanistan, the kind of training that can save lives during combat.

The after action review process provides a forum for everyone on the team to offer critical feedback about the team's performance. It becomes a forward-looking activity as participants suggest potential tactics for improving performance on the battlefield, and define near-term opportunities to pilot those tactics.

In the fragging case, the Army and the US government analyzed the un-ignorable moment defined by the increase in fragging. The Army had built a long history of success through adhering to a strict command-and-control hierarchy. When leaders' decisions were being undermined in this most extreme way, the Army realized that it needed to adapt its organizational culture, to institute some new rules for interaction among its members.

As a former Army Ranger, now a hospital executive, said to us, "People may not be using hand grenades, but fragging occurs in organizations all the time, especially when leaders don't pay attention to those they are responsible for." Tools like the after action review give leaders and associates opportunities to voice and address concerns as part of their everyday work. They facilitate an open discussion of the critical issues the situation raises.[14]

IT'S SYSTEMIC

An un-ignorable moment contains all the information you as a leader need to understand the dynamics of a cultural clash. At University Hospital, all the roles that make up a surgical team were present in the operating room: patient, surgeon, nurses, surgical technician, and assistants. In play was the interaction between an older way of working and a newer one. Team members were working in their roles as they believed they should. It was a microcosm of the clinical culture of the hospital system.

The tensions that surfaced in that incident were not just about a missing sponge or a conflict between two people. University Hospital itself was grappling with needed changes in how it delivered care to patients, as well as changes in the authority structure that would allow all the roles on the surgical team to work together more effectively. Those changes were driven by new health care regulations meant to lower costs and improve the way hospitals throughout the United States deliver health care. Those engaged in the un-ignorable moment were at the tip of an iceberg—their interpersonal interactions were grounded in a system-wide set of cultural challenges in the hospital, in the health care industry, and in society as a whole.

An un-ignorable moment, by unfolding all the information you need to understand a clash of cultures, makes explicit and open for discussion—and alteration—the tacit, unspoken cultural agreements about "the way things get done around here." When such agreements are made explicit, people with direct knowledge of them will be able to answer questions and describe what they are doing and why they are doing it in a specific way.[15]

One of the reasons continuous improvement methods and tools, such as Lean and Six Sigma, are so useful is their ability to make explicit a set of cultural agreements about how to solve a problem. Lean and Six Sigma methods—made famous by companies such as Toyota, Motorola, and General Electric—use a defined set of steps, designed to fit their company's needs, to solve manufacturing problems. One approach to Six Sigma developed by Motorola, for example, is the DMAIC method—for define, measure, analyze, improve, and control—and there are tools to use in each step.[16] A software manufacturer that we'll call Quire (you'll read more about it in Chapter 3) used DMAIC to integrate the cultures of companies they acquired. By designing its own version of the method, Quire created a problem-solving language that could be shared across a company now comprising multiple companies, each of which had its own set of cultural agreements prior to becoming part of Quire.

MANY OF THE SYSTEMS that organizations put in place to get work done, make decisions, and determine how we work with each other become tacit over time. People no longer talk about these systems and cultural agreements; they just follow them. They are often passed down over years and across generations of the business, just as family traditions are passed down, and learned by doing rather than through explicit instruction. When cultural agreements and rules for behavior are tacit, and as a result are not discussed, it's difficult to make what is so familiar, and taken for granted, "strange" enough to be noticeable. That is one reason why start-ups and first-generation businesses sometimes have an advantage over older, multigenerational companies: they have an opportunity to deliberately create a culture and new ways of working together from scratch.

When agreements are tacit, the very things that have contributed to a history of success can get in the way when change is needed. This is often highlighted for those who work across national boundaries, especially when religious, governmental, and other cultural differences between countries are pronounced. Barry experienced this firsthand during his work on a leadership development program in the United Arab Emirates (UAE).

In the late 1990s the political leaders of Dubai, one of the Arab Emirates, had made a risky, farsighted decision to diversify its oil-based economy by becoming a center for trade in the Middle East. The country made large financial investments to expand the capacities of Port Rashid, a major transportation hub, create a world-class airline, and build a new airport. To help manage this growth, Dubai brought in the expertise of executives from England, Australia, Asia, and the United States.

But Dubai could not stake its future on expatriate talent. It needed to equip its own people to manage and lead the rapidly growing businesses and mammoth real estate projects. That's when the Wharton School of Business was called in to design and implement a leadership development initiative called the Dubai World Leaders program that would introduce business skills—marketing, finance, and strategy—as well as leadership approaches. Barry was chosen to be a member of the faculty team.

A hundred young Emiratis, most of whom held executive positions in a variety of companies under the Dubai World umbrella, were invited to participate in the leadership program. They were smart, engaging, and eager to see the country grow, but they were comfortable working within their current cultural agreements. They expected the state to provide schooling and health care. They enjoyed a social milieu of large families living in relative luxury. And they had extensive job opportunities,

presentation. We gave an overview of the competitive landscape, discussed our analysis of the company's performance,
and then went into a detailed review of Murphy's real estate
holdings. We talked about each holding, one by one, and the
current plans for each. As we went along, the leaders began
to whisper to one another. Gradually the whispers turned into
rumbles. This is just what we expected. What we had discovered, and what Murphy's leaders were stunned to realize, was
that Murphy Development was *running out of land*. If all went
according to plan, given the development projects in the pipeline, it would be landless within two years.

This was a stunner—an un-ignorable moment. There had
always been plenty of land and Ryan had been the purchaser.
That was his gift, his expertise, and his primary responsibility.
He had purchased land with great foresight—it could take decades for a market to mature around a property to the point that
development made sense. But attempting to follow the same
strategy within a two-year window would be impossible. Without land, Murphy couldn't develop. But buying land at current
market prices would mean changing its whole cost structure.
Could Murphy survive? This was truly a moment Dan and the
company's leadership could not ignore.

After the retreat, Dan again felt the need to *do something* and
do it immediately. He had just taken over the company, and suddenly the ground had been removed—literally—from beneath
his feet. However, he fought the instinct. He saw that, given the
rising cost of land and the short time frame, his father's strategy
would no longer work. He realized the company needed a new

approach and the only way to develop it was to work closely with his colleagues and do some serious strategic thinking.

Accordingly, Dan, Ian, and Matt got to work. After further analysis, they agreed that the acquisition of land was still critical to the future of the business, but they needed to pursue more complex deals—and they didn't have the expertise to do that. They brought in acquisition experts and people who could help them access capital. They built a new division to assemble a portfolio of land holdings that could be held, developed immediately, or resold. They also developed a few new projects collaborating with a company that had a lot of land but didn't have the expertise in the markets Murphy was strong in. The new experiments represented the kind of risk that Ian and Matt had been encouraging Dan to take; and the risk paid off. Murphy Development gained an extended collection of land parcels they could consider developing and greater flexibility to expand and grow.

For Murphy Development, slowing down enabled the company to speed up. But it took an un-ignorable moment for leaders to see the importance of gaining understanding before taking action.

Leverage the power of stuck. An un-ignorable moment shows that you and your organization are well and truly stuck: you can't go back, you're unable to move forward, and you can barely conduct business as usual. It's an uncomfortable place to be. When you're stuck, you generally want to get unstuck as quickly as possible. That is how Dan Murphy and the executives at Murphy Development felt when they discovered they were running out of land. But it's important to pause long enough to learn from the condition of "stuckness." What is causing the friction? What cultural agreements are in conflict? What ways of working are being challenged? Whose identities are being threatened?

Un-ignorable moments erupt like earthquakes. Cultural conflicts act like the earth's tectonic plates. When two different ways of working meet, they grind away at each other under the surface, neither one giving way. Pressure builds to the point where nothing moves. In an earthquake, the pressure finally becomes so great the plates sharply shift position, releasing the energy in a tremor that shakes the ground sometimes for miles around. In organizations, a similar thing happens. The pressure finally releases itself in a sharp moment that can be felt far and wide.

What's important to understand is that the pressure has usually been building for some time and the un-ignorable moment is an indicator of just how much energy is available to be harnessed—and that's the leadership challenge. Not to tamp the energy down but to draw it out and channel it. Earthquakes topple vulnerable structures and disrupt the landscape, but they can also lead to positive change—communities rebuild, reorganize, and reinvent. Similarly, the tensions and bottlenecks inside your organization can act as a source of creative energy. This is often not the case with places in the organization where everything is running smoothly, everyone feels comfortable, and there are no tensions or pressures. Those places rarely stir up change. As long as the

Emirati in Dubai were satisfied with expatriate leaders and managers, they had no reason to introduce a new set of agreements about how work needed to get done. When that changed, the friction between old and new agreements was inevitable.

To explore the power of stuck, let's return to University Hospital. About a year after the un-ignorable moment, the hospital system was invited to join a national campaign to increase the amount of time nurses spent with patients. Research had shown that nurses were spending as little as 25 to 30 percent of their time devoted directly to patient care, with the bulk of their hours spent on other duties. Andrea Crowley, the chief nursing officer at UH, believed that a key element in improving patient safety was enabling nurses to spend more time with patients. She set a target of 50 percent for the nurses at UH.

Over the course of a year, Crowley and her staff achieved amazing results. Nurses were newly engaged and energized. They collaborated with the supply management staff to improve the way supplies were stocked and organized, so that nurses could access everything they needed more quickly and easily. They worked with the pharmacists to streamline the process of getting medicines and with lab technicians to make it easier for nurses to access test results. By the end of the year, nurses at University Hospital were spending as much as 55 percent of their time with patients at their bedsides. Crowley and her colleagues presented their results at conferences around the country, and other health care systems began picking up on their practices.

Then Crowley decided to expand the initiative to two other hospitals in the UH system. It went nowhere. The new ways of working met with stubborn resistance. You could feel the new ways of working grind against the old ones, and within a month the effort was stuck. Fortunately Crowley didn't rush in to demand that the other hospitals comply with the new work practices. She stepped back, paused, and asked us to help her figure out why there was so much resistance to an initiative that helped nurses do more of what they loved to do.

Use resistance as feedback. We are accustomed to the notion of "change resistance" but there are always reasons underlying the resistance and exploring them can reveal valuable information.

That's why we did some serious participant observation in the other hospitals to find an answer to Crowley's question. We interviewed nurse managers and front line nurses. We spent time with them in their staff meetings, went on rounds with them, and talked with them during patient handoffs at shift changes. They were angry, upset, frustrated. They griped, complained, and sniped.

But the bad feeling also supplied a huge amount of useful information. We learned that the nurses in the other two hospitals were well aware of the challenges nurses faced in getting more time with patients. In fact, over the past several months, they had developed and implemented their own set of processes and systems to enable nurses to get more time at the bedside—and they were already seeing some good results.

They were angry because Crowley seemed to ignore their ideas and wanted to shove the new "UH way" down their throats. The processes she advocated were not compatible with their own innovations, the language was different, and the new ways added unnecessary work that actually took them *away* from the bedside.

That was not all. Many of the nurse managers told us that the new ways of working involved tasks and procedures in which they had no training. For example, they were expected to facilitate open forum meetings to encourage people to propose new practices and improve existing ones. Few nurses were comfortable with this idea. They had no experience in leading meetings of this kind nor were they sure what to do with the flood of ideas that might result. Would they be the ones to say yes or no to new ideas? How could they treat people fairly, and maintain good working relationships with them, but also have to kill their precious brainchildren? Not only did they not have the skills to lead such meetings, they were anxious that, if they bungled the process, they would lose authority, their reputations would be damaged, they would be less effective in leading their groups, and all the gains they had made would be lost. That would certainly not improve patient care.

Lesson learned: resistance usually has useful information in it.

———

WE WORKED WITH CROWLEY and nursing leaders from all three hospitals to develop open forums, create a process for managing the flow of ideas, and establish a set of criteria for evaluating them—so the yes-no decision would not be seen as the whim of the nurse manager. As it turned out, almost all the ideas that came forward fit the criteria. We then worked with Crowley and her team to negotiate agreements with the nursing leadership teams at each hospital. Each team committed to implementing new practices in exchange for the support and development their nurse managers needed to do so effectively on their patient care units. The nurse leaders from each hospital signed the agreement and so did Andrea Crowley.

An amazing number of new ideas emerged that became popular and widespread. The nurses initiated just-in-time management development support to help nurse managers build the group dynamics skills they needed. New practices were woven into existing initiatives wherever possible.

For example, a nurse on one unit was often interrupted while working with one patient by another anxiously ringing the call bell. She'd rush over only to discover there was no emergency. The nurse realized that her patients were anxious and wanted to make sure she was available if they needed her. Given the small amount of time nurses had available for direct bedside care, this made sense. So, the nurse gave her patients her cell phone number. "Call me whenever you need anything or are worried about something," she said. "I'll be there within one minute." What happened surprised her. By making herself more available—and reducing patients' anxiety—she received *fewer* requests for immediate assistance, either on her cell or via the call button. When she presented this idea to the rest of the staff and explained the results, other nurses followed her lead. Then the administration acted on a recommendation to supply nurses with cell phones and print cards with instructions on them to give to patients. The new practice worked beautifully. Patients were more satisfied and felt safer, and the nurses could spend concentrated time with each patient.

What had felt like a concrete wall of resistance began to work more like a continuous improvement feedback loop as the energy that had been applied to devising ways to resist new ways of working was redirected into spreading and improving them. Resistance no longer stood in opposition to spreading new practices; it became part of spreading them.

Within a year, nurses in all of the hospitals in the UH system were spending at least 50 percent of their time with patients at the bedside, and nurses in two hospitals were fast approaching 60 percent.

MAKING THE MOST OF
AN UN-IGNORABLE MOMENT

Much of the information you need to make the most of an un-ignorable moment is hidden in plain sight—contained in "the stories we tell ourselves about ourselves," which is how anthropologist Clifford Geertz defines culture.[17] As a leader, part of your job is to listen to those stories and learn from them. By listening to the stories of the people who experienced the un-ignorable moment in the operating room of University Hospital, for example, we heard a narrative about authority and saw the confusion that ensues when different approaches to authority come into conflict.

Collecting and analyzing stories is similar to gathering performance data and analyzing it to make an investment or a major business decision. One data point does not a pattern make, so multiple sources are needed. There is an important difference, however, between ethnographic fieldwork and other kinds of information analysis. We do not rush to interpret what is happening. Instead, we focus on learning from what others are doing as they do it. For example, one nurse we talked with used the phrase "not invented here" when referring to the new ways of working that Crowley advocated. We might have taken that as a defensive comment and assumed the nurse was being obstinate. Instead, we asked her to say more about what that phrase meant to her, to the nurses' group, and how it fit with their ways of working. That's when the issues about authority and training came out: the new ways literally had not been invented at their hospital and, therefore, really didn't fit their ways of working—especially the equally good ones that they *had* invented there and were delivering good results.

To understand the causes of being stuck, it's necessary to listen in, do significant participant observation, and learn the stories people tell about themselves. Without immersing yourself in the work of others, there is no way you can understand and experience what's happening in the way those you are working with experience it. We like to say that developing a "thick description" of what's happening, in as straightforward a way as possible, should come before any other action, and can guide you toward a useful interpretation of what you find.[18]

Here's how we used ethnographic methods to understand the UH incident:

- Two individuals, in different roles (a surgical tech and the lead surgeon), disagreed with each other, and a third person (the head nurse) stepped in to stabilize the situation.
- Every person we spoke with said that the disagreement evoked unusually strong feelings and completely anomalous actions (e.g., the stapler thrown against the wall in the operating room). Everyone agreed that totally unexpected behaviors were involved.
- Because the surgeon made it plain to those in the operating room that he was "in charge," authority issues were in play. As some people told the story, a front line subordinate had challenged the authority of the leader of the surgical team. (Perhaps this manifested a conflict between new expectations about how people should work with each other in patient safety teams and existing expectations about the importance of deference to authority.)
- The surgical tech felt authorized to stick to his guns about requesting a sponge count and then to take action. That meant there were at least two sources of authority in the room at that moment—the surgeon's and the surgical tech's—which signaled a potential clash of systematic ways for getting work done. As we asked more questions, we discovered that the tech's authority came from the techniques and tasks specified in the Putting Patients

First program (e.g., the checklist) while the surgeon's authority came from his position in the traditional hierarchy.

- The issue of leadership and who was really "in charge" came up in the stories of people who were there. More than one description of the event emphasized the conflict between the kind of leadership that involves a single person with positional authority and the kind of leadership in which any member of the team can take on a leadership role when a task or situation calls for it.

- As we learned more about why the surgical tech acted the way he did, it became clear there was a new set of rules for working with others in the OR with the goal of improving patient safety. And these rules had a secondary effect: they flattened the hierarchy. (*If you see something, say something.*) In that sponge moment, the new rules came into conflict with the long-standing agreements about authority. (*Do you know who I am? I'm a surgeon. I lead the team in this OR.*)

- We know that cultural systems for getting work done rarely change unless they have to, and the pressure to make a change can usually be identified. As we continued our fieldwork and kept listening to stories, we learned from the executive team about the internal pressure to improve patient safety. The Putting Patients First program, the checklist requirement, and the "see something, say something" campaign were all part of the leadership's response to that important challenge. It took an un-ignorable moment for them to see that these well-intended steps also resulted in a fundamental and unexpected challenge to the existing authority structure.

- Finally, building on our work at other hospitals and academic medical centers, we hypothesized that the initiative to improve patient safety was part of a broader response to larger pressures at play in the health care system in the United States—particularly to reduce the cost of patient care while maintaining quality standards. The hospital's attempts to respond to these economic pressures led to the conflict of cultural agreements about how work gets done in delivering care at University Hospital. The cultural challenges had to be addressed, or the economic challenges could not be met.

So, an un-ignorable moment contains all the information you need to understand how cultures in an organization are clashing. But what do you do with that information? How can you open up opportunities for identifying what to do about the clash of cultural agreements?

Face the facts before judging the players. As we begin the task of understanding a situation and identifying potential courses of action, it's important not to make judgments about who or what is right and wrong. Instead, make simple, neutral statements that lay out the plain facts that everybody agrees on. At University Hospital, two people in different roles had a disagreement, and a third stepped in to intervene.

By stating the essentials and eliminating the nonessentials—including, as much as possible, our preconceptions about a given situation—each conversation adds its own color and detail and the description gradually gets "thicker." Eventually, after you've had enough conversations and done enough listening in, you begin to see a rich color image that provides much more understanding than the black-and-white perspective of the original statement.

Be prepared to be surprised. As you begin to find the underlying cultural causes of the moment (through your fieldwork, to use the parlance of ethnography), there are always specific questions that need to be asked and answers that need to be found. However, sticking strictly to a list of questions can get in the way of storytelling. You want each person to tell a personal story in his or her own way. What did she see? What did he hear? What was important about what happened? What words, images, and metaphors do they use in telling the story?

During our conversation with Marco, for example, we had a list of questions to ask. But we also learned by listening in that he expected to be fired, and that he did not believe the administration was straight about its desire for people to say something when they saw something they thought was wrong. Why? Clearly we had hit on something by letting Marco tell his story and relate his feelings.

Use feelings as data. Feelings are data, just as surely as facts are. It's important to recognize that this fieldwork will stir up the feelings of the people you are working with, *and your own, as well.* Feelings and emotions often signal an individual's alignment or conflict with a particular version or aspect of a story. Confusion, for example, may indicate a cultural disagreement between expected outcomes and actual outcomes in a given situation. Anger can speak volumes about what an individual or group might expect to lose as a result of an organizational change.

At University Hospital, the lead nurse, Sheri, said she was "shocked" when Marco challenged Dr. Piersen. This statement, and questions we subsequently asked, helped us understand the hierarchy and chain of command generally followed in an operating room. Similarly, Marco's fear for his job prompted us to ask more about Marco's role, as perceived by him and by others, within that hierarchy.

Capture content in context. For working groups, like the operating team at University Hospital, the context shapes the behavior of individuals in the group. The way a person behaves, talks, and thinks changes in different settings and situations. Each group member is both an individual and a person occupying one or more roles. Dr. Piersen acted as an individual, as a physician, as a surgeon, and as leader of the medical staff. Marco behaved as an individual and as a surgical technician. It is not hard to understand why Dr. Piersen, one of University Hospital's most important surgical assets, would feel entitled to his authority within the operating room. Yet in the context of University Hospital and the new Putting Patients First initiative, it is easy to see why Marco felt empowered to speak up. He saw something, so he said something.

These un-ignorable moments are a shock to the system—both organizationally and personally—but they can enable you to take stock of your current situation and start to shape the future. You can:

- *Set an expectation that getting stuck is not a sign of failure*. Instead, normalize stuckness. Make it clear that in order to meet the challenges that come with relentless change, getting stuck will be normal, even necessary, from time to time. If, after their un-ignorable moment, the leaders at University Hospital had acknowledged that things were stuck, they would have reduced the anxiety that spread rapidly through the hospital. Instead, being stuck was at first seen as a sign of failure—something to be avoided, not discussed. Only after working through what it meant to be stuck, and staying with it, were UH leaders able to see that what began as a major crisis opened up the opportunity for system-wide cultural change.

- *Strengthen the confidence that others have in you to help the organization get beyond stuck*. At University Hospital, Davidian and Crowley learned this lesson the hard way. At first, they wanted to do as little as possible and hoped the problem would disappear. Once they understood that confusion about authority was at the heart of the problem, they realized they had to step up and get engaged—first with each other, then with Dr. Piersen and Dr. Green, and the rest of UH. Everyone was watching—to see what they would do, not what they would say. It was Crowley and Davidian's decision to work together through the confusion of being stuck that inspired confidence.

- *Prepare your organization for un-ignorable moments.* Learn the characteristics of un-ignorable moments and develop a process for dealing with them when they arrive.

How do you learn from an un-ignorable moment quickly enough to make the adaptive cultural changes needed? It's easy to say you should just listen to people tell their stories about themselves and their experience, but that is clearly not enough. The next challenge is putting to work what you learn from the power of being stuck in order to put new cultural practices into action.

CHAPTER 3

A Case of
Adaptive Identity

G ARY EDWARDS'S OFFICE AT QUIRE was large and nicely appointed with leather chairs, fine wood paneling, and photographs of Edwards with notable business leaders and politicians adorning the walls—just what might be expected for the CEO of a Fortune 200 company. No one would mistake this for a hip Silicon Valley outfit with an open floor plan, free locally sourced food, and nap nooks. Nonetheless, Quire Software was an important global company based in North Carolina, with business units and operations in fifteen countries around the globe.

We had been invited to meet with Edwards by Wyatt Stromm, a former colleague and now the chief learning officer at Quire. Wyatt, though, was circumspect about the reason for the meeting. "In your parlance," he said, "Quire has had one of those moments that can't be ignored and is looking for a new way forward. As you may know, Edwards has some big challenges ahead. Of course he has an idea of what he wants to do, but is looking for some counsel about how to implement it."

"Does it have to do with the no-acquisition strategy?" Mal asked.

Wyatt chuckled. "Yes, but not in the way you might think." And that was all he would tell us.

———————

WE HAD DONE OUR DUE DILIGENCE ON QUIRE. The company had been a steady and successful player in the software industry for many years. Then Quire grew quickly over a decade, mostly through acquisition (which is why we asked the question)—buying four other software companies in adjacent market segments, including an e-health company, an optics application enterprise, and two security firms—one in retail security and the other in financial services. The shopping spree put the company out about $12 billion, and in the past few years it had been hard at work paying down its debt and integrating the five companies into one.

Gary Edwards had been hired eight months earlier, after the board eased the former CEO into an unexpectedly early retirement. Edwards was charged with getting the company growing again and taking it to the next level of success. Within two months of his arrival, Edwards had astonished everyone, from his own employees to the Wall Street analysts on the quarterly call, when he announced that Quire had set an ambitious target for itself: double-digit profitable growth within three years. How would the company achieve that highly ambitious goal? "Organically," he said. "We are not planning any major acquisitions in the foreseeable future."

———————

THE DAY OF THE MEETING ARRIVED and we had seated ourselves around a conference table in Edwards's office. Wyatt had made the introductions and we had completed the necessary small talk about careers and shared connections and families and current news.

"Now, let me get right to the point," Edwards said. He was a brisk, compact man in his fifties, fit and full of controlled energy. "You know that I've set an ambitious growth target."

"Double-digit organic growth in three years," Barry said. "Extremely ambitious in this market."

"Yes, but what you don't know," Edwards continued, "is there's a particular urgency behind it."

We looked at Wyatt. What hadn't he told us?

"This was no amped-up boast on my part. And the departure of my predecessor was not exactly what it might have seemed."

We were all ears.

"Indeed, the board had a scare. A wake-up call."

Edwards looked at us as if he assumed we knew what he was talking about. Mal made a supposition.

"The acquirer became an acquisition target?"

Edwards nodded. "Got it in one." He leaned forward. "We're vulnerable. No clear growth path. We've done a good job at becoming more efficient, but everybody knows you can't cut your way to growth. Yes, we're vulnerable. A well-known Indian software group came calling. Made an offer the board could easily refuse. But they had to take action. Their first action was to remind me in no uncertain terms why they offered me this position: they want to see growth and see it quickly. Our stock price has been dropping, and that has to be reversed."

Wow. We let the details of the situation sink in and said nothing for a moment.

Edwards looked to Wyatt. It was his turn.

"You're wondering, of course," Wyatt said, "how we're going to continue to pay down debt, complete what so far has been a successful integration of five very different companies, and accomplish double-digit growth in three short years."

Pregnant pause. Still nothing useful to add or ask.

"I'll put it very simply," Wyatt said. "Six Sigma."

Six Sigma? Hmm. Six Sigma is a set of tools and practices widely used in companies large and small to reduce waste, cut costs, and increase efficiency.

"Six Sigma." Barry repeated the term as if to affirm that's what Edwards really meant.

"Yes," Edwards said, unclasping his arms. "But a very particular application of Six Sigma." He leaned forward again, with a gleam in his eye. "Six Sigma *for growth*. Not cost cutting. Not waste reduction. Not process efficiency. Six Sigma for Growth. SSFG."

There was a soft knock on the door. Edwards's administrative assistant, Raylene, poked her head in. "They're ready for you."

Edwards nodded, excused himself, and was gone. Wyatt picked up the thread.

"It's not a crazy idea," he said. "Quire has had fantastic success with Six Sigma. Not just for cost-cutting and debt reduction. But for integrating the companies, too. It has provided a common, consistent language for people across what were very disparate companies when we acquired them. We've used it as a common approach to problem solving. And to figure out ways to work together."

"That's understandable," Barry said. "Especially since all the companies are basically engineering cultures, right?"

"Oh yes," Wyatt said, smiling. "For sure. They all speak tech."

"So now you want to apply the Six Sigma methods to achieve organic growth," Mal said.

"Precisely, but there are challenges." Wyatt explained that when Edwards arrived, he had looked across the company for opportunities and he kept hearing about Six Sigma successes. He began asking if this success could be applied to growth initiatives. Some said yes. Others said no, Six Sigma has run its course. It had become too bureaucratic and would stifle the kind of entrepreneurial activity needed now. This is partly code for how expensive Six Sigma has been—each business unit has to pick up the tab for the Six Sigma support it gets from the central organization.

"I think we can deal with all of that," Wyatt said. "But there's an even more fundamental issue that needs to be addressed."

To both of us, the issue was obvious. "You're talking about a major cultural shift," Mal said.

"Yes," Wyatt agreed. He smiled. "That's why we need your help. We have one hundred days to see if this can work."

―――――――――

WE TALKED A LITTLE MORE WITH WYATT about the cultural shift that would be required. How do you change ways of working in an engineering firm that has built itself into a global power-house through acquisition, integration, and a relentless focus on efficiency? We would need all of our ethnographic tools and cultural change methods, and we agreed with Wyatt that we would start by meeting with the people at the heart of the issue: the Six Sigma leadership team. Did they believe Six Sigma could be adapted to an organic growth strategy? If so, how?

What this group had to say would be crucial. If we could get that group on board, the approach might have a chance. If not . . . things would be a lot more difficult.

Wyatt got us on the agenda of his next Six Sigma leadership team meeting, and we flew to North Carolina the day before to prepare. We were excited yet nervous about discussing the SSFG plan with this group, and we were counting on Wyatt to introduce us and get the conversation started. That was not what happened. An hour before the meeting, Wyatt called. Edwards had summoned him. He would try to get to the meeting, but it was doubtful. We should plunge ahead without him. *Good luck.*

There we were at a brief meet-and-greet social gathering before the formal meeting. Two northeast-based ethnographers mixing it up with fifteen or so engineers, mostly men with southern roots. Informally dressed. Smart. Down to earth. Finely tuned social skills. We had no trouble joining the conversation. We started with family, food, and football. Then we moved on to a discussion of their roles and disciplines, as well as the companies they had been with before being folded into Quire. Clearly Quire had multiple organizational cultures within it—engineering groups with their own cultural norms and ways of working, sales and marketing experts, and folks in the learning organization—teachers, trainers, and organizational development people. The legacy companies had their own cultural norms and histories. In fact, even a decade after an acquisition, in-the-know Quire people could easily identify who had come from which of the legacy companies.

We made it through the social hour and the getting-to-know-you conversations pretty much intact and started to relax about the meeting, since we would at least have a few familiar faces in the room.

Mary Gladhill, the team leader, opened the session and previewed the agenda. We were up first. We started with a few remarks about the importance of Six Sigma to Quire's past success and about the concept of applying the Six Sigma approach to achieving organic growth. We previewed what we hoped to accomplish in the next hour, and asked if there were any questions before we got started.

"Yeah, I've got a question," Gladhill piped up. "Do you guys have experience in software development?"

It was a reasonable thing to ask, although it sounded more like a challenge than a question.

There was no way around it. "No," Mal said. "We have no direct knowledge of what you do. But we have worked with companies with strong engineering cultures. Just not in software development."

"And we do, of course, understand the world of management," Barry added. "And, in particular, the world of change management. We understand that very well."

Gladhill looked completely unconvinced. "Wrong answer," she said. "How can you advise us if you don't know the industry? I'm not against bringing in outside expertise. But look, we have the next hundred days to test whether Six Sigma can be useful in supporting and locating growth opportunities. We don't have time to futz around with people who don't get it."

Time to come up with something.

"Listen," Mal said. "We understand the pressure you're under. And I can understand your skepticism as well. But you have all the software development expertise you need, sitting right here in this room. What you don't have, as I understand it, is a way to come up with growth opportunities. We have helped many other companies—without having experience in their special expertise—do just that."

Gladhill remained silent. She looked at the members of the group.

"Let me add to that," Barry said. "We strongly believe there are opportunities for growth lurking in your organization, waiting to be discovered. We call them found pilots, and we can help you identify them. They can help you find the future you want. You just have to know where to look. We won't be the ones who decide which ones you go forward with. That would take specific expertise. But we can help you get results."

"Yes," Mal agreed. "Listen. Gary Edwards and Wyatt Stromm are very eager to get your support for this effort. Here we are. We've got an hour together. Let's see what we can come up with."

Gladhill looked at her group. She couldn't exactly kick us out of the room, especially after Mal had invoked the names of the CEO and the CLO.

"Give it your best shot," Gladhill said.

Given the circumstances, we decided to forgo a formal presentation and dove right into the work. We asked the group one straightforward question: "Are there people, units, projects, or programs that already exist in the company that are using Six Sigma in any way to find new business opportunities for the company's existing software capabilities?"

They all looked at us blankly.

"Think about the tools you use in Six Sigma," Mal said. Fortunately, Wyatt had given us a crash course in Six Sigma methods, and we had talked about which ones might be best aligned with growth opportunities.

"For example," Barry went on. "What about 'the voice of the customer' or 'customer care-abouts,'" he said, naming two of the Six Sigma tools we had identified as having growth potential. "Are they being applied in ways that might lead to organic growth initiatives?"

"These found pilots don't have to be fully formed new offerings," Mal said. "A found pilot can be a smart person with a brilliant idea. A small team recombining existing offerings in a new way."

"Could be business development people coming back with a customer request for an integrated solution, not just a product," Barry said.

Now we looked at them. It was the moment of truth. Based on our work with many other companies, we knew there had to be found pilots at Quire. Would the engineers collaborate with us—who knew almost nothing about software development?

Gladhill's commitment to the company overcame her skepticism about us. "Yeah," she said. "I've got one." She gave an excellent example—a tiny project pursued by a colleague of hers in a distant corner of the company that she thought could be the seed of a great customer-facing business—if Quire had been in the business of innovation and organic growth. Now they were. Mal grabbed a marker, wrote the project name on a Post-it note, and stuck it on the wall.

That opened the floodgates. Forty-five minutes later, the wall was plastered with Post-its, each with a found pilot marked on it, and names and locations attached. When no more hands shot up, we reviewed what we had. There was a lot of potential on that board. But, as one of the engineers pointed out, it was still just potential.

"This is fascinating and all," he said. "But what do these people, initiatives, workgroups, and events really add up to? There's always a bunch of stuff going on in this company that doesn't go anywhere. Experiments and such."

Another person, from a different legacy company, spoke up. "Besides, I really question whether Six Sigma is the right approach for growth. If these found pilots as you call them are so hot, why haven't they already taken off?"

Fair points. We talked further with the team about found pilots and how their value is constructed. Found pilots are part of a transitional zone—in this case, the zone between using Six Sigma for efficiency and using it to support and stimulate growth. When found pilots don't take off, it's because there's no method in place for working with them to help them realize their potential. It takes skill and leadership to create the centripetal force that helps take the ideas and action in a found pilot and use them to attract the attention, resources, and related ideas that are needed to go from a single idea to a full-fledged new practice. And that will likely be true for Six Sigma for Growth found pilots, too.

The only way to assess the potential of these found pilots is to investigate them thoroughly and then make a judgment about which will be able to contribute to SSFG. We asked the group to do that, with our help, over the next several weeks.

Once again, the group looked hesitant. More work on top of an already onerous workload. An assignment from outsiders with no knowledge of software and no real commitment to the company. But . . . they had to come up with something. And . . . Quire's senior leaders were paying attention.

"Sure," Gladhill said, at last. "We can do that." She looked at her team members. "Can't we?"

Small head nods and quiet murmurs of "I suppose so."

We wasted no time. In the remaining ten minutes we worked with the team to select the found pilots we wanted to evaluate from among the candidates on the wall. We chose three from each of Quire's five business units.

Just as we were wrapping up, Wyatt stuck his head in the door.

"How's everything going?" he asked.

Gladhill shook her head with resignation. "We're all going on a hunt for something called found pilots," she said, with just a touch of the acerbity she was known for and had so effectively demonstrated already.

We took it as a good sign that everybody in the room laughed.

———

OVER THE NEXT SEVEN WEEKS OR SO we conducted fieldwork with members of the leadership team to observe the fifteen found pilot candidates in action. Many of them, of course, were operating under the radar. The projects were fragments. Informal. Sometimes a little disorganized. But they were exciting and encouraging and once we poked our noses into one, we usually learned about others the leadership team didn't yet know about.

Quire had more than 70,000 employees working in its five business divisions around the globe; it would be surprising if there were *not* multiple initiatives going on in different business units working on different approaches to similar problems. But the senior executives had mostly been looking outside for new growth ideas and concepts, often at their competitors. They counted on their internal operations to develop complete product and service offerings and only saw them once they were fully formed and ready for the market. That's one reason why they had they not been able to see the future that already existed in fragments right in front of them.

At the end of each week, we got on the phone with the Six Sigma leadership team to share what we had learned and plan ahead for the upcoming week. At the end of the fourth week, we hit pay dirt.

The consumer electronics rep on the Six Sigma team told us about a found pilot that he thought had exceptional potential. It was a knowledge management (KM) system that an engineer in Quire's consumer electronics business was working on. At that time, the field of knowledge management was in transition. KM had been associated with information organization and warehousing. Now people were working to transform KM into a just-in-time learning system that would enable people to access knowledge about what they needed, when they needed it—no longer an information vault but a dynamic, two-way knowledge and experience sharing resource. Since 2004, this is exactly what has happened, and we now take KM systems for granted.[1] Back then, however, it was a wide-open field with unlimited growth potential.

Scott James, a consumer electronics engineer, was the genius behind their KM concept. He was working on algorithms that people could use to access knowledge within and across Quire's multibillion-dollar consumer electronics business quickly, engagingly, and with access to a richer store of knowledge than ever before.

The rep from the optics business jumped in as soon as the consumer electronics rep finished describing the KM project. He had come across another pilot that might bring a new dimension to James's work. This one was the brainchild of a learning expert, Jill Norris, based in the optics business, who was using social network analysis to connect people who had similar interests or were searching for a particular kind of knowledge within the company. Knowledge management algorithms could help everyone in the network locate everything currently known about that topic. Jill was a well-known native North Carolinian with an extensive network that she used thoughtfully. Her challenge was that she had been unable to get people in the company to pay attention to the power of network analysis. Most engineers thought it was fluff.

What if these two got together? They might be able to combine their ideas into a powerful knowledge management and sharing solution that could be marketed internally to Quire, and to all kinds of organizations around the world. Looked like a great growth opportunity. The electronics and optics reps promised to get James and Norris together.

WE IDENTIFIED MANY MORE found pilots with commercial potential, enough to give us confidence that the Six Sigma for Growth approach could probably work. We were cautiously optimistic. Wyatt was encouraging and supportive but also let us know that word of this "found pilot thing" had gotten out. How could it not, with the Six Sigma team snooping around the nooks and crannies of all five business units?

Some of the five business unit leaders were intrigued by the efforts. They were feeling the heat from Edwards, who was looking to each of them to come up with a business plan that demonstrated how, and how much, their businesses would contribute to the double-digit growth target. At least three of the five were hopeful that SSFG would help them meet their goal. Of the other two unit leaders, one was on the fence and the other was "not enthusiastic," as Wyatt put it.

Even so, about two and a half months into our engagement with Quire, Wyatt concluded that we had gathered enough evidence that Six Sigma for Growth could work, and the time had come to share the news with the CEO. Gary Edwards was encouraged by what he heard. He gave Wyatt the green light to move forward into the second phase. At the same time, Edwards wanted to make sure that Wyatt didn't lose the utility of Six Sigma for cutting costs and improving efficiency. We worked with Wyatt to lay out the next steps. The first task would be to assemble a coalition of people who would lead the SSFG initiative without drawing away all the talent from the traditional Six Sigma organization.

For that, we would need a strong leader. It couldn't be Wyatt himself, and it certainly couldn't be an outsider. Wyatt had just the person for the job: Gus Miller. Wyatt had selected Miller to head up the original Six Sigma operation and report directly to him. "He's an old Six Sigma Black Belt, a well-respected engineer, and something of a cowboy," Wyatt told us. "He knows how to shake things up inside this company. He's got ingenuity, tons of experience, and a really broad network of relationships. Plus, Edwards likes him. They worked together on a software industry task force a few years back. They got along like two peas in a pod."

OFF WE WENT AGAIN TO NORTH CAROLINA, this time to meet with Gus. He already had some ideas about how to assemble a coalition, who should be included, and what they should do. He had also come up with some new language.

"I'd prefer to call these found pilot things 'proof points,' if that's all right with you gentlemen," Miller said. "'Found pilots' sounds just a wee bit . . . academic, maybe? Jargony? I think we'll get greater understanding and have better luck with proof points. Each one will be a kind of proof that Six Sigma can help stimulate growth."

No argument from us. We too liked the sound of "proof points."

Gus Miller, we learned, strongly believed that Six Sigma was the key to achieving organic growth. "The language is familiar to everybody," he said. "Everybody understands the steps and the behaviors. I believe it can help build bridges from where we are now to where we want to be. It's not going to be easy, but I think it's our best way forward."

We talked at length about the SSFG effort. Miller understood that the move from efficiency to growth represented a major cultural shift. Earlier in his career he had gone through just such a change at another company.

"It really affects everything you do," he said. "It doesn't mean that Six Sigma isn't still important for improving efficiency. But those focusing on growth will have to revisit the everyday choices they make. "How should I use my time today? What am I not going to do?"

"For sure," Barry said. "It affects all your decisions. Who are you going to partner with? What meetings should you attend? Which ones can you skip?"

"How will we allocate resources?" Miller added.

"If you've been through it, you know how uncomfortable a shift like this can be," Mal said. "You're asking people to reinvent themselves. I'm sure that people who have been successful in this culture, which has been devoted to increasing efficiency for so long, are going to have some difficulty adapting to the demands of rapid organic growth."

Miller smiled. "Damn right, so let's talk about the who," he said. "We need to get all five businesses involved, even though some of their leaders aren't quite on board yet. If any of 'em feel ignored, that will come back to bite us. At the same time, if those guys get too involved and make a lot of noise, the doubters might feel like their reps are getting a little ahead of themselves—and of the business."

"That sounds right," Mal said.

"Now." Miller lowered his voice. "I need to alert you to one little situation."

"What's that?" Barry asked.

"Mr. Norbert Ball," Miller said. "Bert Ball. Or Bertie as his closest friends, of which he does not have a huge quantity, call him. Bert leads the supply chain management software unit, which, as I'm sure you gentlemen know, is the biggest, most profitable, and most successful in every way unit in the company. Bert is a huge fan of Six Sigma and has used it brilliantly to make his operation as lean and mean as you can imagine. But, and this is a big but, he thinks Six Sigma for Growth is a load of bunk. Doesn't think the tools apply. Doesn't think it can help identify growth opportunities. In fact, he thinks it could lead to all kinds of problems. Disrupt the good things we have going. Take us down some very deep rabbit holes. And end up thwarting the very growth path we want the company to take."

Miller let this news sink in for a moment.

"Having said all that," he continued. "I don't want you gentlemen to worry. Just don't mess with Norbert Ball. Let me handle him."

With that in mind, we spent the next couple of hours with Miller putting together a detailed road map for developing the coalition and defining its roles and goals. Toward the end of our conversation we asked Gus how he would define success for the first year of work. He was quiet for some time. We waited.

At last Miller spoke. "I've thought about that quite a lot," he said. "There is one metric that I think would be most meaningful."

"What is it?" Mal asked.

"To have Gary Edwards make a bold, definitive, and very public statement about SSFG. I want him to let the Quire world know, in no uncertain terms, that he supports the program. And that he believes it is integral to Quire's success as a company." He looked at us. "That would really be something. If he did that, I'd be pretty satisfied."

"But I thought he is already a supporter," Mal said. "Wasn't this in large part his idea?"

"Yes, it was, but Gary can only put his public support behind two or three things in any given year or two. Right now our work has been pretty much under the radar. Wyatt's face is on it, but Gary is waiting to see what will happen. And if he steps up and makes a public statement, that means we have most of the business unit presidents behind us. Gary won't go public with his support for SSFG unless they are with the program.

"What I'm trying to say is that if our CEO makes a clear and public statement that Six Sigma for Growth is the horse he wants Quire to ride to stimulate growth, lots of other things will have happened to make that possible. Sounds simple—but it's not. We have a lot of work to do."

"Is there a good opportunity for him to make a statement like that?" Barry asked.

"Sure," Miller replied. "The annual meeting of Quire's Six Sigma organization in November. Gary's slotted in to give the keynote. That would be a killer moment."

We heartily agreed.

"So," Miller said. "Let's get to work."

WITHIN A WEEK, Gus Miller started building his SSFG coalition. He met with the heads of Quire's businesses and asked each of them to nominate a person to serve on the coalition. We had agreed on some basic criteria. The people had to be senior in experience, trained in Six Sigma, widely respected, with strong social networks and significant influence. They had to be go-to people that others in the business relied on to help solve difficult problems. And, most importantly, the nominees would ideally be champions of one or more of the found pilots—or proof points.

Miller knew he was asking the business leaders to commit to Six Sigma in two ways. First, they would be pledging the time and energy of one of their people to the coalition. Second, they were symbolically aligning their businesses with the SSFG effort, at a time when they were under pressure to deliver performance results.

All was going well until Miller had his meeting with Norbert Ball. He had saved Ball for last so he could demonstrate that the other businesses were supporting the SSFG idea and had volunteered a person to serve on the coalition.

Norbert Ball was not impressed. "I don't have anybody I can spare for this wild goose chase," Ball said to Miller. "We've got a successful business to run. And a company to prop up."

Miller did not take the bait. He was not expecting Ball to come around to SSFG and wasn't going to try to convince him. All he wanted from Ball was to not stand in the way—and to allow one of his people to serve on the coalition.

"Well, I understand you're pretty busy, Bert," Gus said. "And I know how you feel about this project."

"It's a crock," Norbert said, just in case there was any doubt in Miller's mind. "You know how hard I've worked to get my people aligned behind Six Sigma. I can't, and I won't, ask them to switch gears and use the same tools for growth. It's too confusing and cuts against what I'm trying to accomplish here. Besides, we're already growing fast, faster than any other unit in this company. We have three new projects in the pipeline that could set us up for the double-digit growth target."

"That's fantastic," Miller said.

"And I hope to eventually convince you that SSFG can help the rest of us catch up to you," Gus continued.

"Plus, I will tell you that I have no great faith in our Mr. Edwards to achieve double-digit growth even if you find a thousand organic growth opportunities," Norbert said. "I'm willing to bet he won't be here long enough to see his vision through."

"Well," Miller replied, "that's quite another discussion that I'd be happy to have with you some other time. But for now, I have a very simple request."

Norbert made a small harrumphing noise. "What is it?"

"Well, Bert, you remember that partnership you wanted to pursue with that Chinese supply chain group about nine years ago?"

"Sure." Norbert's face clouded over. He suspected where this was going.

"You remember, I'll be willing to bet, that you didn't have much support among the senior management team for that adventure."

"No," he admitted. "They hated the idea. Especially our beloved ex-CEO."

"That's right." Miller paused for a moment. "But the partnership got approved. Along with a pretty hefty budget."

"Yes it did."

"Do you recall how it was that our CEO changed his mind?"

"You convinced him."

"I helped convince him. Because I thought the partnership was a good idea. And that you weren't getting a fair hearing. Even though you were being a pain in the butt about it."

"So this is payback time?"

"I prefer to think of it as an exchange of social capital, Norbert," Miller said. "That partnership wasn't the only time I've spoken up for one of your unpopular projects. All I'm asking is that you not publicly denounce this one until we have a chance to prove it out."

"I see." Norbert did not look pleased, but he also did not seem to have any way out.

"And," Gus added, "let us have one of your people. Three months. That's all we ask."

"Okay," Norbert said. "Just do me one favor."

"What's that?"

"If this initiative tanks and Quire ends up getting sold and chopped into pieces, don't come running to me for a job."

Miller smiled. "Deal."

WITHIN TWO WEEKS, Miller had his people in place: five senior people, one from each of the business units, two of his own

Six Sigma team, and himself as leader. From our first meeting with the group, it was clear that the process of identifying and selecting proof points for further development would be easier said than done. The coalition members knew a lot about what cost-cutting looked like but were less sure about how to identify a growth opportunity. It didn't take long for them to admit that they felt uncertain about how to proceed, where to look, or what they were really looking for. They felt stuck.

That's when we introduced them to our fieldwork methods, including listening in, participant observation, and shadowing. We talked about where found pilots ("proof points" to their way of thinking) could usually be found—on the edges and the front lines, in the ideas of new people, and in initiatives or situations that made them uncomfortable.

———————

ONE FIELD VISIT STANDS OUT in our minds because it demonstrated to us just how deeply ingrained and accepted Six Sigma was in this company. The coalition team met every three weeks, rotating locations from one of Quire's businesses to the next. This allowed us to put participant observation and Six Sigma tools into action with them. One meeting was held in the Midwest and included a tour of a facility where Quire's proprietary software was installed into point-of-sale data systems for retail stores to provide transaction security. Here we were able to see the physical evidence of Six Sigma at work in the company.

You know how it is when you have learned about an approach through secondary sources to the point that you think you understand it pretty well. Then you encounter it in action and it takes on a whole new meaning. That's what happened for us on this facility tour. We saw immaculate clean rooms and assembly areas carefully laid out for greatest efficiency. Charts on the walls displayed process improvement projects as well as listing "intelligent practices." Gus pointed out to us who the Six Sigma experts were and how they were working with the managers on the floor. Watching them observe as they made rounds of the production sites, facilitating team meetings, drawing process flow diagrams on the white boards, and asking good probing questions—you could see how they contributed to the company's operations.

Six Sigma was visually embedded in the ways of thinking and working at that facility. It became even clearer why Gus was convinced that it made sense for Quire to use its "old" cultural agreements about how work gets done as an incubator for new cultural agreements. As Jon Katzenbach has pointed out, "You can't trade your company's culture in as if it were a used car." He argues persuasively that it is better to build on the cultural assets you have than to reinvent them. [2] At the same time, we had another reaction to what we saw. We referenced earlier the truism that the strongest cultures are the ones that find it most difficult to change—and we saw plenty of evidence that Quire had a very strong culture. Shifting the emphasis of this engineering culture from efficiency alone to efficiency *and* growth was going to be a significant challenge.

Just before we left the factory, we sat in on a business development meeting where a team of folks from across the business were doing a deep dive about ideas for new product development. There were people in the room from marketing and sales, finance, industrial design, and programming, and a member of Gus's coalition facilitated the group. Participants focused sharply on generating business opportunities—what new products could they quickly bring to market that would be attractive to their customers? There was a lot of give-and-take, and the group generated a lot of ideas. Most wouldn't see the light of day, but a few might be worth taking forward. We left on an upbeat note.

This experience reminded us once again—and demonstrated to the coalition team—the value of getting out into the field, looking inside everyday work, spending time on the front line, working alongside middle managers, and sitting in on the deliberations of executive teams.

Engaging in fieldwork also helped allay the concerns of some coalition members. *Are the found pilots we've discovered anomalies? Can we really start small and build to critical mass? Will they show us how the future kinds of behavior we need are already showing up in the present?* The more found pilots they discovered, the more they saw that new ways of working with Six Sigma in the service of growth were evident within and across the businesses. Now they faced the bigger challenge of coordinating and supporting the interest that the found pilots were beginning to generate (even though the team had not officially gone public yet)—and the expectations that were beginning to mount. To do that, they had to mobilize the energy of people throughout the organization.

———————

WE WERE FORTUNATE that the Six Sigma process was deeply ingrained in company culture and was an asset they could draw on. As coalition members began to talk up organic growth within their businesses, they used a familiar language to tackle new problems. Each coalition member met with the unit leadership team, and usually the business development team, to walk through the Six Sigma for Growth tools. Then they would work together to identify people and places inside the business and some external customers where the team could put Six Sigma for Growth tools to work. Six Sigma became a bridge, a transitional device that leaders could use to cross from the past to the future.

As the Six Sigma for Growth work progressed, the coalition met every six weeks and reported on the progress of at least two found pilots for growth. A cluster of opportunities around security emerged in a few of the businesses—products and services that would improve a company's ability to protect customer data wherever it was held.

The Six Sigma group for the retail business unit built on a practice it had tried once before with some success—bringing together a number of customers for a workshop to look at barriers to security and potential ways to overcome those barriers. This practice was risky, as some customers were competitors.

But they were willing to share experiences in areas where they were stuck and to brainstorm together about common problems. Quire's agreement with their customers was that no business development or sales people from Quire would be in the room, and there would be no pitches for any of Quire's products or services made. This generated some anger and frustration inside the retail business, but their president agreed to go along with the experiment.

The Six Sigma team used tools like "voice of the customer" to draw out their customers' points of view about the problems they faced, and then worked with them to create a "common operating picture" of what success would look like if those problems were addressed. They used one of our tools, "back-casting," to create a road map to the future. This involved iden-tifying the obstacles they would encounter along the way, and ways of overcoming them, in order to achieve success.

The process worked well for Quire, bringing it together with customers it had not engaged with for some time. Quire learned a great deal about the data security worries of the big retail outfits, and the opportunities for new offerings that could address them. The Six Sigma team then fed this data back to its product devel-opment teams. Within a few months, Quire began to see an uptick in interest and eventually an increased flow of orders for data security products, which it was updating based on the knowledge and trust gained from the workshop. This success even got the attention of Norbert Ball, who put in a call to Gus Miller.

"This will knock you back," Norbert said, "but I'm calling about the Six Sigma for Growth thing."

"Wow. Really? Well, your guy on the coalition is doing a great job. Thanks for sparing him."

"No need to coddle me, Gus. Listen, I've heard some good things about the data security and compliance workshops. That area sounds promising."

"It would be even better if we could get some real participation from you guys in supply chain. Set up a program of some kind."

"Whoa, slow down, Gus," Norbert said. "Let's not get ahead of ourselves. I'm not quite ready to champion this stuff. I'm just saying it sounds interesting."

"By the way," Miller said, following a hunch. "Are you on track for double-digit growth? How are those three projects coming along?"

Norbert cleared his throat. "We've had a couple of hiccups," he said. "Nothing catastrophic, but they're not performing quite as we had hoped. We had to shut one of them down."

"Just wondering. I know the security people are planning to scale up soon and are looking for a collaborator."

"You're transparent, Miller," Norbert said.

"Never said I wasn't."

"Have them call me," Norbert said. "Sorry, got to go. I have another call."

Miller smiled. If Norbert Ball got on board, everybody would soon know about it. That would be a major win.

BY FALL, THE MOOD AT QUIRE had changed. Word about Norbert Ball had indeed gotten out. Miller and Wyatt, and even Edwards, began hearing bits of feedback that the business unit leaders were getting behind the Six Sigma for Growth effort. Maybe it could contribute to delivering the organic growth results they were looking for. The buzz was loud and positive enough that Wyatt suggested to Edwards that we get together to discuss further action.

"Thanks for coming in," Gary Edwards said as he turned away from his computer to greet us. "It's good timing, or bad timing, depending on how you look at it. The board just got our latest quarterly report. It shows we're on track for 4 percent growth for the year. That's 4 percent higher than this time last year. But apparently it's not good enough. I just got off the phone with one of my board members, John Broome. He says we can do better. Wants to see double-digit growth *this* year. I told him three. That was the plan. He couldn't really say much, but he wasn't happy. And he's my fourth director call today."

"That's odd," Wyatt said. "Why so much concern? Four percent growth is fantastic compared to where you're coming from."

"It's because they got another acquisition offer. Excuse me, a potential 'merger.' Code for 'we would like to swallow you up.' As I think I said to you guys, that will happen over my dead body. It will have to come to a vote, but I think I can keep the wolves away for a while longer."

"Do you still think the three-year target is achievable?" Wyatt asked.

"It's a definite maybe. We've had some wins this year. But 4 percent this year does not guarantee 8 percent next year."

"What do you think about the contribution SSFG has made so far?" Barry asked.

"Another certain uncertainty. Some of those initiatives have contributed to our growth this year. But can these things really scale to become major longer-term winners? That I don't know. And can we count on SSFG to keep on finding new opportunities? That's a real question mark."

"I think it can," Wyatt said.

"Part of the answer to your questions has to come from you," Mal said. "If you're committed, people will make it work. And if Six Sigma takes you part way there, they'll work hard to figure out what's next. If you show ambivalence, they'll pull back."

"Yeah, I know that," Edwards said. "What do you suggest?"

"Get your business unit leaders together," Barry said. "Put the question to them. First of all, are they really committed to the organic growth strategy? If so, are they willing to put their money on SSFG as one of the drivers of growth? If not, what else have they got up their sleeves?"

"I could do that," Edwards said. "But what about Bert? Where does he stand? There's no point getting four guys behind this if the leader of our biggest business says forget it."

"Gus tells me that Mr. Ball may have had a slight change of heart," Wyatt said. "I think it's worth the risk. If you can get the other four leaders behind you, even if Bert remains neutral, it's worth it."

Edwards tapped his nose for a moment, then came to a decision. "Let's do it. I'll get them together."

WE WERE NOT PRIVY to the meeting Edwards held with his senior team about ten days later. Gus Miller was not invited. Wyatt Stromm, dealing with a problem in Europe, also had to wait to hear the results. He got a call from Edwards around midnight. The meeting had run for six hours, through dinner, and had just concluded. Edwards was cautiously optimistic. Four of the five business unit heads had taken the SSFG pledge of support. Norbert Ball remained neutral. It wasn't an overwhelming mandate, but it wasn't rejection either. What's the next step, Edwards had wanted to know. The next morning, Wyatt called us with the same question.

That's when we remembered Gus Miller's success metric.

"Edwards needs to make a public commitment to SSFG that the whole company will hear and take seriously," Mal said.

"What are you thinking?" Wyatt asked.

"That Gus Miller had it all figured out," Barry said. "The November meeting of the Six Sigma group. Edwards makes SSFG the cornerstone of his keynote address."

We could hear Wyatt gulp on the other end of the conference line.

"That should do it," he said. "One way or the other."

THE BIG EVENING ARRIVED: the annual meeting of the entire
Quire Six Sigma organization. All the Six Sigma people from the
businesses—twenty-five to thirty each—were there. Another ten
people from the central Six Sigma operation. Wyatt's Six Sigma
leadership team was on hand. And all five business presidents.
A few members of the industry press had also been invited and
sat in the back of the room with their laptops at the ready. Some
two hundred people had packed into the hotel ballroom for an
evening of awards, recognition, speeches, congratulations, self-
promotions, good-natured joking, and serious direction setting.

Before the awards ceremony, Edwards took the stage for his
keynote remarks. The Six Sigma team held its collective breath,
waiting to hear what Edwards had to say about the SSFG initiative: an interesting experiment that had not yielded sufficient
results to keep it going for another year? Would he mention the
program at all? Maybe he'd just sidestep the whole thing.

As it turned out, Edwards went wide and deep. He recommit-
ted to the organic growth strategy. Reiterated the goal of double-
digit growth within three years. Highlighted the substantial contribution Six Sigma had made to Quire's success in the past. Said
that the revitalized version, Six Sigma for Growth, had demonstrated tremendous potential for identifying and scaling up opportunities that were already proving themselves inside the company.
He challenged everybody in the room to redouble their efforts in
finding new ways forward for the company they cared so much
about. He spoke with conviction, enthusiasm, eloquence.

It was a milestone moment. Un-ignorable. You could almost
feel the tension between the two cultures being released in a

sudden burst of positive energy. The applause was thunderous, at least by the standards of software engineers.

After the speech, Edwards grabbed us, Wyatt, and Gus Miller and pulled us into a side room. What was up? Edwards was jubilant and thanked us for the work we had done on SSFG. But his manner betrayed an underlying sense of urgency.

"Has something happened?" Wyatt asked.

Edwards shook his head ruefully. "I guess you could say so," he confessed. "Our friend Norbert Ball has reverted to his more characteristic behavior."

"What do you mean?" Mal asked.

"He has been talking to some board members on the side," Edwards said. "He wants to spin off the supply chain business. Make it an independent entity. He's trying to convince board members that it could increase Quire's shareholder value because the market would reward a supply chain pure play. And, of course, the IPO would have him at the helm."

"Whoa," Miller said. "That would put a big dent in Quire."

"It wouldn't help," Edwards agreed. "I don't know if Bert is serious. Maybe he's just gunning for my job. Whatever, the board is breathing down my neck harder than ever. If we don't make this organic growth thing work. . ."

He looked at each of us, one by one. "We've started the cultural shift. I can feel it. The question is, can it happen fast enough to achieve this ambitious growth target? If not, maybe I should start working to change the board's expectations. Or maybe we need a Plan B. Maybe we *should* spin off the supply chain business. Let Norbert grow the unit by acquisition and efficient integration, while the rest of us take the new course. Maybe getting smaller is the best route to getting stronger and more profitable."

He clearly did not expect an answer to his questions at that moment.

"One thing I'm sure of," he said. "We're not going back to the old ways. The company has an incredible new sense of energy, even in the conflicts and debates we're having. We still have the best of what we had, that engineering culture, and Six Sigma can help us maintain our efficiencies. But it can also help us focus our growth efforts in a whole new way. I don't know what you guys think, but I find it exciting."

He patted Wyatt on the shoulder, shook hands with the two of us (Mal and Barry), and gave Gus a fist bump. "Now I'd better get back into the fray."

CODA: THREE YEARS LATER, Quire achieved a growth rate of 10.1 percent. The supply chain management business stayed in the fold and delivered a 12 percent growth rate. Norbert Ball saw how several of his organization's SSFG projects became supercharged when they were injected with ideas, talent, and technical resources from other business units. Mal and Barry worked with Quire through several more engagements, becoming close colleagues with Wyatt and Gus. Gary Edwards, who had been CEO, was voted into the additional position of chairman of the board.

CHAPTER 4

Finding the Future Inside

I T MAY SEEM ODD TO TALK ABOUT the power of being stuck. But being in the stuck condition is a great place to find a way forward. Does the solution we need, the future we're trying to create, already exist somewhere in our organization right now? Almost always, the answer will be yes.

This is not to say that finding the future inside your own organization is easy. As we experienced at Quire, it can be difficult to see what's happening inside your own culture. It's all too familiar, all too "natural." As a result, it is easy to overlook the seeds of a company's future success ready to grow and blossom. When you ask, "Where is the future already happening?" you launch an investigation of useful assets—people, places, events, and projects—that are usually hiding in plain sight.

You will not find the future whole, but in fragments. It might be an IT manager who is successfully keeping her internal customer's costs down. A business unit that has developed a novel approach to working cross-functionally to accelerate product development. A customer service team that discovers a new way to make life easier for customers and build their loyalty as a result. Two departments at a university that have lowered the barriers to interdisciplinary collaboration. Such fragments may look insignificant in the context of the larger organization, but the behaviors required to do things differently in these kinds of activities can show the way to a different future. As science fiction writer William Gibson put it, "The future is already here, it's just not evenly distributed."[1]

In the previous chapter, we introduced the concept of found pilots—these very useful fragments of the future—in the story of Quire. Now we'll explore the characteristics of found pilots, how to search for them, and where they are mostly likely to show up.

FOUND PILOTS ARE MORE than just good ideas or promising activities. In fact, they can't earn the designation "found pilots" until they pass an important test: they must demonstrate how they put new working agreements into action and do so in ways that others can put into action, too. You can think of them as "transitional objects" because they not only show the way to the future but also help people make the cultural shift from one set of agreements to another.[2]

We refer to these future fragments as "found" because they are usually tucked away in the corners of the organization, operating under the radar, so small or so new that few people know about them, and must therefore be discovered. They're not usually created through a formal program or by an executive mandate. They don't necessarily appear on an organizational chart or a calendar of events, or the agenda of regularly scheduled meetings. They need to be searched out, brought to light, and leveraged. They are like pieces of a jigsaw puzzle you're working on, but without the picture on the box to guide you.

We use the word "pilots" because these activities are usually small-scale experiments, trials of new ideas and tests of alternative ways of getting work done. You could say that Marco, the scrub tech at University Hospital, was conducting an informal and highly personal pilot when he threw himself across the patient; he was testing a new behavior. Dr. Green, too, was involved in a pilot that he led and invented with his surgical team.

Because these fragments of the future must be discovered and because they are one-off or small-scale experiments, they often go unnoticed for a long time, sometimes forever. When you discover them, you'll find they contain flashes of insight about the future; they show how processes might work differently and carry a great deal of information about what works and what doesn't. They are raw material that can be shaped and leveraged to create buzz, attract others, and move a change initiative toward desired results.

A Dorm Room Solution to
a Campus Computing Problem

Let's see what a found pilot looked like in an educational institution we'll call Ivy University. During the Internet boom of
the 1990s, Ivy U was facing a challenge common among educational institutions at the time—how to support the exponential
growth in computer usage across campus. But Ivy U faced a significant twist to that challenge. The university had a centralized
IT function while the institution itself was highly decentralized.
There were, for example, four different email systems running
on campus. Decisions about information technology were made
by people scattered over many administrative departments,
student centers across the university, and in departments of
the many different schools—such as engineering, business, the
medical school, and the College of Arts and Sciences.

Most of the decisions weren't made by people at central IT,
who represented fewer than half those working in information
technology jobs across the institution. Individual schools and
administrative departments were responsible for supporting
their computer users. Central IT was responsible for what it
called "the glue functions"—the systems holding everything
together, such as registration and finance—and for working
with the schools and departments to keep everything up and
running.

With so much decentralization, the IT function faced a challenge not unknown to other centralized IT organizations: how
to provide customers with the service they needed in a timely

way, while ensuring that important standards for security were not compromised and costs were kept under control.

As you can imagine, the schools and departments with the most resources wanted to control the user experience with the latest email package, presentation software, and classroom technology. And each of the schools and staff departments wanted to do what was needed when it was needed, not when central IT decided the time was right. Believing their particular needs to be both urgent and important, they often tried to figure out their own work-arounds to the problems they faced. This, of course, led to lots of wasted effort and no small amount of tension.

Jane Winthrop, who led the central IT group, had to figure out how to build a stronger relationship with the colleges and administrative departments but didn't know how. She decided to bring all the stakeholders together and try to figure it out, and asked us to help design the big get-together.

We recommended that Winthrop charge this group as a task force and ask a faculty member to cochair it with her. Together, they recruited twenty-eight IT people and also invited eight nontechnical faculty members to join. Winthrop was shocked when all eight agreed. "They're usually the last to get involved in anything they consider to be 'administrivia,'" she said. "Perhaps we're on to something important here."

The meeting convened. Around the table sat key people from all the major schools and administrative departments. There were even a couple of student government representatives. Winthrop set up the task they were to tackle: determine the role of the central IT department and the role of the schools and other departments in supporting computer use across campus. In other words, the objective was to negotiate an agreement about who was going to do what, and agree on what each was willing to give up to make it happen.

Over a series of half-day meetings, we worked with the task force to identify where members' interests differed and where they aligned. Then, in order to promote divergent thinking and explore options that engaged everyone, we invited the group to self-select into small groups to construct new models for computing support based on their interests. They developed four computing support models; at the third meeting we tested each one against difficult situations to see if central IT and the decentralized schools and departments could hold each other accountable to make the models work when the going got tough.

After testing the models, everyone agreed that only one of the four met their expectations. It was a model that put the user at the center: each person in the university community would have, in effect, "a computing home"—faculty, administrative staff, students, everyone. If it worked, people could take all their computing questions to their computing home and get help whenever they needed it. No longer would a monolithic central IT organization try to tell everyone what to do or try to be everything to everybody. And each person would—somehow—have easy access to support that was close by, immediate, available 24/7, expert, and even a pleasure to deal with.

It was an appealing vision, but it meant having front line support when needed as needed—just in time. The task force

members came to an agreement that the schools and departments would work locally to provide the frontline support.
Central IT would work at the enterprise-wide level to provide
systems support, data administration, and services for schools
and staff departments.

The challenge was to figure out how to make it all happen.
The task force considered, and rejected, several approaches to
creating a computing home—including the creation of a large
internal network, installation of complex software applications,
and turning over the support function to an IT outsourcer. These
were all expensive and resource intensive, and none of them
seemed quite right for an institution that prided itself on solving
its own problems. No one could agree on which way to go.

After trying on and rejecting these and other approaches, the
task force was beginning to lose steam. Members were getting
frustrated and testy, pointing out the flaws in each other's ideas.
At one meeting, Professor Kurt Felcroft, a faculty member from
the engineering department, began bickering with the dean of
students, suggesting that this was ending up like all the other
interdepartmental groups he'd been part of, a complete waste of
time, where no one was willing to budge to make things work.
"It's easy to think together at 50,000 feet," Felcroft said. "Now
we're talking about central supporting us in a new and different
way without taking away our autonomy, and there's nothing but
silence about how we'll make it work from our end."

It was clear in that meeting, in that moment, that Winthrop
didn't know what to do. In the past they had used the traditional four-part engineering approach to put new IT models

in place: analyze the organization's work processes, redesign them, put them back together again, and then get people used to the changes. This time was different, and they had come to genuine agreement, even if was at 50,000 feet—and now it was all about to fall apart. When the meeting ended, the disgruntled participants hurried out of the room.

Between that meeting and the next we worked with Winthrop to see what could be salvaged. She said she had truly believed that getting the right people in the room would lead to the right result. They were all smart people, and they all knew what had to happen, that was clear. And she didn't think it was as simple a problem as Professor Felcroft described. They were in uncharted territory, and no one knew exactly what to do. She asked if we had any recommendations.

We suggested that she build the next meeting around two questions: *Where does the solution already exist? Where is the future already happening in your organization right now?* Again and again, we had learned in our work with clients that the future is already manifesting itself somewhere inside the institution. Just as we had done with the people at Quire, we urged Winthrop to keep the task force but change the task. They should work together to try to identify people, initiatives, and places where the kind of frontline support they needed was already happening, and where other people were moving forward in a way that modeled the decentralized-centralized approach they were working toward. It's easy to remember that moment—Winthrop looked at us as if we had two heads. But we pressed on, and she agreed to give it a shot at the next meeting.

When the next meeting arrived, we reminded the task force that it had already accomplished a great deal. That many diverse groups never get as far as agreeing on a computing support model that works for everyone. We reminded members that they had worked through alternative models, and that the "computing home" model met their criteria for success and stood up to the test cases for accountability they had put it through. We suggested that, as Winthrop had stated at our last meeting, they were charting a new course into unknown terrain. Charting such a course is difficult, but people can incrementally act their way to new thinking instead of believing they should be able to figure it out completely all at once. If the latter is possible, they'd already be doing it. So far, no one had left the room.

We then put the same question to this group that we asked at Quire: Where is it already happening? That's when Robin Trestle, one of the students on the task force, spoke up for the first time. "Most of the problems I have happen late at night, and I just go to the guy on my floor who helps everybody out when they run into computer problems." The other student member of the task force, Mia Singh, immediately agreed. "We never use the central support desk. There are enough geeks in the dorms who like to troubleshoot and strut their stuff. Sometimes they compete among themselves to see who knows the most."

Up to this point the conversation had focused on faculty and staff. If having a computing home really applied to the whole community, students would need computing support when they needed it, where they needed it. This would be worth following up on.

One of the faculty members, George Cavalero, jumped into the conversation, saying he was impressed with what he heard from Robin and Mia. Cavalero went on to describe an initiative he was chairing sponsored by the College of Arts and Sciences (CAS). They were trying to turn the dorms and student houses into hotbeds of intellectual activity, living/learning environments where students could use computers to connect to ideas and to each other 24/7. To do that would require computing support. CAS leaders had struggled to find a solution. Should they set up a help desk in the basement? Hire squads of independent contractors? "Now," Cavalero said, "I realize the solution has been right there all along, staring me in the face." He said he had been hoping to get something useful out of his participation in this task force, and now he'd found it.

These are just two of many found pilot candidates that emerged during the meeting. None of them was fully baked, and task force members agreed to follow up on them between meetings and to look for others as well.

At the next meeting, there was a different energy in the room. Cavalero reported on the fieldwork he had done in the dorms with Robin and Mia. The dorm geeks clearly would need some training and coordination to avoid compromising security protocols. But they were passionate about computers and very skilled troubleshooters, even if some of their techniques were unorthodox. Winthrop suggested that central IT use work-study money to hire and train them, and Cavalero proposed that they share the cost and use this new "geek team" for frontline support for the CAS living/learning initiative, too. They were taking found pilots and beginning to shape them in ways that were making a difference.

This turned out to be one of a number of solutions, none of them perfect, that the task force decided to work with as they moved forward. They put together a sub-group to launch and monitor a number of experiments, the geek team being one. They also decided to run central IT like a public utility with an advisory board composed of representatives from the different schools, staff departments, and student councils. The task force also came up with the idea that central IT should sell its services where a market existed. Under the new model, schools were responsible for the frontline support of their own members. They could provide it themselves or buy it from each other or from central IT.

As the experiments took off, so did the connections between the two partial solutions to create a computing home for every student—the College of Arts and Sciences' living/learning initiative and the tech-savvy students in the dorms who were already helping their friends. Central IT hired the student geeks and gave them supervision, tools, and training. The students providing frontline support expanded their reputation as a team of go-to tech support gurus, coordinating with each other as well as with CAS and central IT. Clearly they were proud of their identity as the geek team.

As the initiative unfolded, the university learned new approaches for tech support from watching students help other students, and applied what they learned to other computing homes for faculty and staff across the campus. As the schools and administrative departments took more responsibility for developing their own tech support teams, the role of central IT shifted, too. It focused its mission, stopped giving direct support to end users, and closed the walk-in help office. It supported the colleges and departments, which in turn supported their computer users—central IT supported the supporters. Support included everything from providing forums where people could share expertise across the university to volume discounts on software applications across schools. And the College of Arts and Sciences developed a stronger, more practical living/learning initiative, with the on-the-ground computing support it needed to be successful.

We learned a great deal from this project about the power of found pilots as guideposts to the future—because found pilots don't come fully formed, they're easy to overlook. It helps to have the a microcosm of the entire system in one room together—in this case the twenty-eight members of the task force representing different parts of the university system. That way people can spark each other's thinking, and it's easier to discover a possible fragment of the future, pay attention to it, and flesh it out. Cavalero recognized that Robin and Mia had said something important; otherwise, the task force might have overlooked the value of dorm geeks.

We also learned, as we had so many times before, that people know a lot more than they think they do. After the initial shock of being asked, "Where is it already happening?," people in all sorts of organizations are able to come up with people, places, events, and projects that are piloting the future in the present.

Characteristics of Found Pilots

The people engaged in found pilots are often on the leading edge of future ways of working. Jay Bradner, a young cancer researcher who heads a team at his lab at Harvard Medical School and the Dana Farber Cancer Institute in Boston, is a leader in his field. Jay has identified a molecule that may interrupt the growth of certain cancer cells and may lead to breakthroughs in cancer research. But he is not conducting his research in the traditional fashion. Rather than patenting his discovery and trying to capitalize on it, for himself and his institutions, he is giving it away through an open source approach to drug development, asking colleagues to work with the molecule and see what they learn. The ultimate goal is to accelerate the development of cancer treatments.[3] Bradner's behavior is farsighted yet not all that unusual. It's a way of working we have begun to see in fields ranging from biomedical research to software development to innovations in the social service sector.

PEOPLE SUCH AS BRADNER are innovators or mavericks who work in ways that are aligned with the future that their organizations or disciplines are trying to create. Bradner is not just following his personal passion or doing what he believes is right. He understands the context of biomedical research and the goals organizations are trying to achieve—how large academic institutions do science, and why that process moves so slowly. And he knows how protective pharmaceutical companies can be with their proprietary compounds, sometimes even preventing the spread of knowledge. So he is trying to work against the grain within both these cultures by inviting others to accelerate research and open up these discoveries so one company cannot own and control them. Innovators like Bradner are trying on new ways of working to get results that propel cancer research in a new strategic direction. It pays to nurture, learn from, and champion them.

Dan Murphy brought a similar spirit to Murphy Development when he succeeded his father, Ryan, as CEO. Some years after Dan and his colleagues discovered they were running out of land to develop—in their own un-ignorable moment—Dan was trying to continue the turnaround he had started, but he recognized that significant work would be required to get the company where he wanted to take it. Dan knew the company had a lot of strengths to draw on, but significant organizational change was needed for it to become more performance-driven and competitive. Like many family businesses, change was slow inside Murphy Development. Loyalty to employees ran deep, sometimes to the detriment of speed and innovation.

We worked with Dan to organize a grassroots change program to address these issues, with the ultimate purpose of keeping what was strong about the company, making it a great place to work and a successful business for many years, while promoting change where it needed to happen. Our strategy was to engage employees at multiple levels in uncovering Murphy's cultural assets and figuring out how to strengthen and build on them.

The process began with Dan identifying a coalition of mid-level leaders to run the program. These were junior managers who were already taking on leadership roles and had strong potential to handle more. We met with this task force several times and, with Dan's guidance, set them to work. They began by listening in to groups across the company's several divisions—through interviews and observation, surveys, and focus groups—to try and identify cultural traits that made Murphy Development distinctive, embodied what it stood for in ways that gave it an edge. They translated these traits into an identity statement about being "a family company" along with a set of values—innovation, quality, teamwork, integrity—and named this effort the Murphy Challenge.

We, probably like you, tend to be wary of cultural improvement programs when they show up as slogans or catch phrases. But there was real enthusiasm here, and people were willing to link these ideas to real behaviors—to get serious about implementing the values. On the one hand they wanted to applaud values that worked, while also being clear about those that no longer fit—for example, giving people a job for life, regardless of their performance, or not challenging current ways of doing things. At this stage in the life of the company, they needed to encourage new ways of doing things and then make those new behaviors routine. The group took on the important challenge of fostering an environment that was both family-based and focused on business results, to be achieved in part through new behaviors promoting accountability. And this was all being done as the business was growing exponentially, making an informal face-to-face culture difficult to sustain, with employees spread out over a broader geography.

The next phase of the Murphy Challenge was to identify found pilots—places across the company where individuals or groups were already "living into these values" in exemplary ways. Some of the found pilots were selected to become projects on a broader, company-wide scale. Some were small and modest but no less important—such as implementing new safety practices on construction sites, or improving the buying experience for their strip mall tenants. Others were larger, like expanding a customer service program for their new medical office division.

We went through three rounds of this work—with a range of projects launched across the company at the end of each round. The results were significant on a number of fronts: quality improved, stronger connections were forged between divisions of the company that were usually quite isolated, and a cohort of young leaders emerged and gained visibility within the company. Culture became a lever to accelerate growth of the business, to improve service to Murphy's customers, and by doing so gain significant competitive advantage in the markets they served.

After many years of working with organizational cultures, we have come to believe that cultural initiatives like the Murphy Challenge are incredibly important, especially when they draw on hidden assets and valuable resources in found pilots. The people who lead them—people who are creating the future—put their passion and energy to work because they *want* to, not because they are coerced. When leaders show their commitment to maintaining the strengths of their company's identity while taking on the challenge of change, they attract other people who also become personally engaged. Their projects and activities unlock energy that can be applied to innovation and change—in ways that are aligned with the direction they want the entire organization to go.

Best of all, the energy of found pilots is not a scarce resource—unlike time or money. As we saw at Ivy U and Quire, the harder you look for found pilots, the more you find. Jane Winthrop and her university-wide task force located student computer geeks working in one of the dorms and discovered that they were part of a broad network of students helping other students solve computer problems. Then they discovered that the College of Arts and Sciences needed computer support to make its living/learning community campaign successful, and things built from there.

———————

FOUND PILOTS OFTEN SURFACE in teams whose members are working together informally, "off the grid," experimenting with new ideas and new ways of accomplishing tasks more efficiently. People bring ideas to their teams; other team members then modify and improve them as they apply them to their everyday work.

A study of molecular biologists by Kevin Dunbar, for example, found that breakthroughs usually occurred around a table in weekly meetings, not when scientists worked in isolation. "The results of one person's reasoning became the input to another person's reasoning . . . resulting in significant changes in all aspects of the way the research was conducted."[4]

Found pilots can be difficult to see because teams often meet in what sociologist Ray Oldenburg calls a "third place," an environment outside the office or home that is conducive to connection and interaction.[5] In his book *Where Good Ideas Come From*, Steven Johnson provides many examples of Enlightenment-era ideas that emerged from third places, such as coffeehouses in eighteenth-century Europe.[6] The current interest in "coworking spaces" where freelancers gather and collaborate is a modern version of the eighteenth-century coffeehouse.[7]

For a modern-day example, consider Riverton, Inc., a consumer products company in the Midwest. While working with Riverton, we learned that a group of middle managers got together once a month for an informal dinner, each time at a different restaurant. What was their purpose? To talk about the role of "middles" in improving overall company performance—and to act as a support group when difficulties arose.

The group invited Mal to join it one evening. He found that it included not only current but former middle managers, "alumni" who had gone on to jobs in other companies. The group had been gathering for more than a year, and evidently no one else at Riverton knew about the get-togethers. Mal certainly hadn't before being invited, and he had been working with

Riverton off and on for several years. In this unpressured third place setting, they had come up with a handful of intriguing ideas. They would bring the most promising ones to their formal management team meetings and some had been implemented.

One of the things the "middles" found most irritating at Riverton was the annual employee engagement survey. Employee satisfaction had been declining steadily for three years, and everyone on the management team agreed that the survey in its current form wasn't working. The survey asked employees for suggestions that would boost the company's performance on its values. These values had been articulated by the leadership team and raised in various communications efforts. *Integrity. Respect. Passion.* For two or three years, middle managers had dutifully compiled employee recommendations and suggested ways Riverton could make improvements, but they were rarely, if ever, implemented. As a result, the survey had become a "check the box" procedure and a waste of time. Middle managers had to deal with growing employee frustration while their leaders kept demanding they improve employee morale.

The "middles" came up with a new approach at one of their dinners. Why not build the values discussion into the performance review process? Any manager with direct reports should ask during the review conversation, "How have you experienced the company values in your everyday working life?" The middles suggested beginning with "respect." This was a novel and simple approach—asking people what the values meant to them and how they already played out in work situations (and how they did not), rather than surveying them for new ideas about how to implement the values.

The idea was well received by the executive team, and Lucas Halvorson, Riverton's CEO, was particularly enthusiastic about it. He had championed the values initiative in the first place and had been disappointed by the way it had gone so far.

The new approach was implemented and people responded positively, so the middles pushed the idea further. Why not invite the managers to collect stories from the performance reviews and share them at their management team meetings? They might also gather the stories together into ebooks and start a blog where anyone could put up a story about experiencing one of the values in action.

That, too, was done. People at all levels were swept into the conversation about values. The conversation encouraged new value-oriented behaviors. The values came to be seen as real and grew stronger. An idea that started as a scribble on a napkin at the middles' dinner had become a transformative initiative.

———

JUST AS FOUND PILOTS gain energy from off-the-grid settings, the ideas generated are often mash-ups and recombinations of existing ideas—a process that takes something known into a new and unexplored place. Like the unlimited energy that pours from found pilots, the raw material to fuel them is abundant. People creating the future have the ability to look at available

The concept of positive deviance originated in work on children's nutrition done by Tufts University professor Marian Zeitlin.[10] Researchers Jerry and Monique Sternin applied the concept in their work with the Vietnamese government in the 1990s. At the time, there was an epidemic of childhood malnutrition in that country; some two-thirds of the children were starving. Many outsiders had come to Vietnam and proposed solutions to the problem, but all had failed. But the Sternins took a found pilot approach.[11] Working with community volunteers, they visited families in extremely poor villages, looking for children who had healthy body weight. When they found such kids, they investigated the families further, trying to determine what was behind the difference. They found that the families of the healthy kids were practicing culturally deviant behaviors, ignoring the standard practices of what to eat and when to eat it. Through participant observation, the Sternins saw that the norm was for kids to eat a diet composed mostly of rice. But rice was in short supply and also lacked necessary nutrients. The positively deviant families were able to supplement their rice diet with greens and shrimp, good sources of nutrients and protein. In some families, the kids ate multiple small meals throughout the day, so they had a more frequent and consistent intake than the undernourished children.

The families of the well-nourished kids were the found pilots for the Sternins in their efforts to change nutrition in Vietnam. The solutions were hidden in plain sight in the current practices of some members of these Vietnamese village communities. Like all found pilots, they were born of necessity, created by people who were solving problems in ways that made sense to them. They were not elaborate programs proposed by outsiders and did not require extensive resources to support. The elements of the diet were a kind of obtainium and the way they were put together was nutritional *bricolage.*

Found pilots are usually social activities. They recombine and build on existing raw material, including the ideas people have; they are positive and deviant at the same time. As a result, the current cultural system for getting work done tends not to reject these new ways of working. They fit current cultural norms well enough, while stretching them in a new direction. Other families in the Vietnamese villages, for example, did not see what the healthy families were doing as radical or strange. It was easy for other to adopt these practices because they so closely resembled their own eating habits. The Sternins first had to find those people who were piloting new ways of gathering food and eating it. After they discovered what these villagers were doing and learned how they did it, the Sternins and their Vietnamese colleagues shared that information widely and taught others how to find greens and shrimp to supplement their diet. Once they understood the connection between the deviant eating habits and healthy children, Vietnamese villagers began adopting the new approach.

How to Discover Found Pilots

As Yogi Berra famously said, "You can observe a lot just by watching." And you can learn a lot about found pilots through various kinds of participant observation, such as listening in, shadowing, and action learning. Whether it's the example of Dr. Green at University Hospital, the dorm geeks at Ivy U, or Wyatt and Gus at Quire, the goal of listening in and participant observation is not to conduct a commando raid on the found pilot and to interrogate its members for information, but rather to participate in the group, to observe what happens as its members work.

As you participate and observe, you ask questions about how the work is being done and why things are happening the way they are. You will find important hidden meaning along the way, but first you want to focus on the action. What exactly are people doing? Why are they doing it in this particular way? These observations will yield much greater understanding than asking people to talk about their work outside of the work setting, as in an interview. You have to be there, paying attention, and the work has to be going on for you to understand how it deviates in useful ways from current ways of working.

SHADOWING TAKES THE TECHNIQUES of listening in one step further by focusing on roles and how people do their jobs. The participant observer follows a person over a longer period of time—a day, a week, maybe more—observing, asking questions, and noting observations. Then they share insights with others involved in the change effort.

Shadowing can be done peer to peer, with others in the same role, or across roles, functions, and locations. Shadowing is a great way to break down silos and connect parts of an organization to each other and to the whole, simply by learning what others do and why. The shadower brings fresh eyes to work patterns that have become so ingrained that those who engage in them can scarcely see them anymore, let alone question or change them. In short, shadowing can make visible the tacit aspects of culture.

About a year or so after the un-ignorable moment at University Hospital, Andrea Crowley and Dr. Davidian asked for help with their ongoing effort to improve the quality of patient care while reducing its cost. They had already cut costs to the bone and now had to rethink how work was done to make any further progress. Doing more with less had reached its limits. We recommended inviting nurse managers and frontline nurses to shadow each other as a way to begin thinking differently, rather than creating another project to cut costs or improve quality. They had way too many projects as it was. People were already overloaded. Shadowing could be a way to bring fresh eyes to ingrained work patterns.

We decided to work with people who were in the thick of the action every day—nurse leaders and managers and clinical specialists—and trained them in basic fieldwork techniques. The nurses spent a good number of hours over a period of eight weeks observing their colleagues on their own patient care units, and in other units as well. They found the experience eye-opening. The participants came up with a long list of ways to improve care while reducing cost—such as including family members (not just physicians and nurses) in patient rounds to make sure they were receiving information and support that they needed; improving signage on the unit so visitors didn't wander around confused; and having a dedicated computer to create up-to-the-moment internal IT capability on each unit.

Perhaps most important, frontline nurses and middle managers gained a deeper understanding of each others' roles. They came to realize that frontline nurses could and would take on more responsibility, which in turn freed up middle managers to spend more time leading further improvements on the floors. A self-sustaining positive-reinforcement cycle had begun. After the shadowing work was completed, one of the nurse leaders observed, "This activity is far more beneficial to the creative problem-solving business needed to implement the new patient care model than a prescribed amount of time managing the nursing unit." Based on the success of this experience, nursing leaders have shared shadowing methodology with other units, and a number of related activities have sprung up organically, including a journaling club that nurses have set up to share their recorded experiences. Individuals are pairing up to shadow each other outside of the formal program as well, and find it easy to implement many of their ideas right away.

Each of the ideas they recommended was already in action in one place or another on patient care units, and they had observed many of them in their shadowing activities. Observing the work of colleagues with fresh eyes, using an ethnographic lens, made it possible to see and appreciate found pilots that were hidden in plain sight. Ideas, practices, and behaviors that had been tacit—*that's just how we do it*—became the ingredients for new ways of working system-wide, once they were made explicit.

ACTION LEARNING COMBINES organizational learning with applied work on real projects. It allows participants to try out new ideas and methods in the field—in the natural "laboratories" of their offices, conference rooms, research centers, and factory floors—where the learning starts to happen, then step back and reflect on what they did and the knowledge they acquired—a cycle of learning and action. Participant observation methods can be integrated into action learning to help leaders discover found pilots in one part of the business that can be used to accelerate growth in other parts.

While working on an intensive leadership development program for a global pharmaceutical company, we saw the powerful benefits of combining action learning and ethnography in the pursuit of found pilots. The leaders of "Pharmactic" knew they had to be out in front of the movement among pharmaceutical companies to reduce health care costs for their customers. If they failed, they would lose business to companies that succeeded. They also knew they'd have to partner with hospitals to make it work, and they needed some fresh ideas on how to do that. Barry worked with them to design an action learning program for this initiative. As part of that work he trained some of their leaders in participant observation techniques—helping them learn how to listen in to their own organizations, scouting and discovering existing ideas and projects that were aligned with the changing direction of the company.

Team members reached out to their colleagues and identified several company initiatives in locations around the world where they were partnering with hospitals and other health care providers in innovative ways to lower health care costs. They saw an opportunity to learn from work their colleagues were doing in India on a microbial product that some larger hospitals were using, and where they were achieving exciting initial results avoiding infections and readmissions. The action learning team connected with their colleagues and explored this found pilot—observing how nurses used the product and interviewing doctors and company reps. Then they took lessons learned from India and applied them to the introduction of similar products in another important emerging market country. This form of ethnographic action learning opened up a new way of working within Pharmatic that in turn created opportunities for increased sales and stronger relationships with customers.

WHERE TO LOOK FOR FOUND PILOTS

It's not always easy to find these harbingers of the future within your organization, but they tend to show up in some interesting places: at the edges and on the front lines, in the words and actions of new people to the organization, and in things that startle or unsettle you.

At the edges and on the front lines. Found pilots can often be found at what we think of as the edges of an organization's activity. Edges can take different forms, but an edge always stands in contrast to the core. The core focuses on the ways work traditionally gets done—based on current agreements that are usually tacit and taken for granted. Edges include the people and places where new ways of working often show up. One kind of edge can be close to the customer while distant from the core in the way field offices can be distant from corporate headquarters. Frontline workers work at that kind of edge, distant from where executive decisions are made, but often directly in contact with customers who can provide feedback and new ideas.

Another kind of edge, where the inside of the company meets the outside, is occupied by those who work with suppliers, outsiders who sometimes learn enough about a company over time to be valuable sources of alternative ways of working. A manufacturer of battery-powered tools, for example, discovered that a company supplying it with batteries had streamlined its manufacturing process in ways that reduced production costs while speeding up cycle time. The founder of the tool company became interested in what his supplier was doing and asked them to train one of his teams in ways to streamline the tool manufacturing process. By working at the edge with his supplier, our client was able to discover found pilots that eventually led to a long-term partnership between the two companies that has helped each improve productivity and increase revenue growth.

Found pilots operating at the edges act as heralds of the future. A wonderful example of this occurred when an executive at Hewlett Packard, one of the largest manufacturers of desktop printers, was settling his daughter into her dorm room for her first year of college. He suggested they visit the campus bookstore and pick up a printer. She said that wouldn't be necessary. "I don't really print anything out anymore." In that comment, the executive caught a worrisome glimpse of the future of the computer printing business and a harbinger of some big changes coming.

Creative experiments at the edges of your organization don't happen in a vacuum. They often emerge in reaction to current ways of working that are the norm in the core of the organization. It can be tempting to grab new and exciting things you learn from found pilots at the edges and drag them into the core immediately. But the core represents the status quo, and its inertia can be powerful. There is an emerging body of social science research on the relationship between the edge and the core.[12] It shows that if you want your company to try on new ways of working, bringing the core to the edge can be more effective than taking the edge to the core. This is what the power tool company leader did when he took one of his production teams to his supplier for training in ways to streamline the production process. The core represents the status quo, and the edge is designed to test it.

We feel similarly about found pilots. You are best served by exploring and learning from found pilots before developing them further. Don't rush to incorporate new ways of working into the mainstream. They are weak signals at first and not strong enough to affect the existing system for getting work done. Remember, the current cultural system took a while to establish itself. If you bring the edge (found pilots) to the core (current ways of working) too quickly, you'll likely create confusion and generate resistance. That's what happened when Marco Fierro encountered Dr. Piersen in the operating room at University Hospital. The top team had announced new ways of working through the Putting Patients First training but was not prepared for the consequences.

We mentioned earlier that people working on the front line function at the boundary between your company and its customers. This is an edge worth singling out for special attention. Working directly with customers puts those at the front line in a privileged position to anticipate new practices that are about to take hold and put them to work long before others even hear about them. They feel the pull of the customer, who sees the product or service in use, and often have to adapt in the moment in order to respond to customer needs.

Malcolm Gladwell coined the phrase "cool hunters" for people who go undercover to tap into trends and emerging fads. They infiltrate the edge of fashion, music, and culture—and report back with information about new trends and products.[13] People at the front line don't have to go under cover. They can be "cool hunters" as part of their everyday job—if you let them know it is part of their job—and tap into what they are learning.

In the words and actions of new people. You probably have heard an aphorism attributed to the great hockey player Wayne Gretzky: the secret to success is not to skate to where the puck is but to where the puck is heading. New people are often hired because they bring ideas and skills needed to take a company where the puck is heading, not where it is today. Think about those who have recently joined your organization and how they differ from people who are already there. What have these people done elsewhere, and what are they doing now that could solve chronic and entrenched problems? How are recent customers different from past customers? What turnover have you seen in leadership, and what stimulated the change? Changes in hiring, customer base, and leadership may be lead indicators of where your organization is going—and can lead you to found pilots.

For instance, an influential professional scientific society was searching for its next CEO. Rather than hiring a seasoned association management executive, as one might expect, it brought in a business-minded leader from a global chemical producer. This decision was a highly visible step toward a new future for the association, in which it acted more entrepreneurially and partnered more actively with industry, and saw the global stage as its playing field. We see it at our own firm as well, when we debate the roots of our past versus the emerging possibilities of our future. Should we hire a finance specialist, a psychologist, or a social scientist, given our roots in these disciplines? Or someone with expert knowledge in a particular market that we want to penetrate? At a small firm like ours, each new hire is a bet about the direction we believe we need to head in order to grow and adapt to the changing markets we serve.

Things that startle or unsettle you. Being startled, surprised, frustrated, or bored can be an indicator that you are encountering a set of cultural norms or working agreements that differ from your own. Listen to yourself. Pay attention to what has startled or surprised or made you uncomfortable lately. When have you felt unsettled? What caused it? Something new and interesting may be happening there.

The friction of the new can trigger surprise or frustration. It can be a signal that something different may be worth paying more attention to—not because you have to agree with it but because it's an alternative way of solving a problem, making a decision, or getting work done. These deviations may be practices that you want to look at more carefully and potentially keep if they help you move toward the future you're trying to create.

For example, the work of Dr. Green and his surgical team represented a new way of working that University Hospital initially didn't find interesting. Dr. Piersen had more influence and generated greater revenue. Listening in helped us see that Dr. Green was using checklists and tracking results in ways that foreshadowed the need for a new system for getting work done in the operating room in order to improve patient safety and control costs. Just as important, though, was *how* Dr. Green and the nurses and technicians were working together— the cultural rules they had established for working with each other as an interprofessional team, including their agreements

about where and how authority and responsibility were distributed. The more we listened in, the more we heard that many
people knew about Dr. Green's team and liked what they heard.
Dr. Green and his team were one of those found pilots that was
a weak signal until the UH leadership team discovered that he
was making patient safety a priority in ways that the hospital
needed to see a lot more of.

The patient safety problem was not just a system-wide patient safety problem—it was a system-wide cultural problem.
The good news was that parts of the future that UH executives
wanted to put in place already existed on Dr. Green's team. The
bad news was that existing UH cultural practices conflicted with
the new ways of working. Dr. Green's team had to practice under the radar for quite a while because there were no supports in
place to encourage and sustain their new working agreements.

Final Thoughts on Found Pilots

Leaders of organizations that want to change strategic direction
don't always realize they must change agreements system-wide
for how work gets done and for how people work with each
other to get it done. In other words, turning strategy into action
is a cultural challenge. Fortunately, your culture is a renewable
resource.

The raw material for culture change is all around us in the
form of found pilots, already emerging inside the organization
and in its relationships with customers, suppliers, and the wider
environment. We have seen that found pilots are more likely to

be successful if they come from inside, often from the edges. Because people regularly resist practices imported from outside, found pilots from inside or close to the inside of your organization will have greater impact and are more likely to be accepted. They fit the existing culture while introducing new ways of getting things done at the same time.

We began this chapter by suggesting that identifying, exploring, and learning from found pilots can help organizations harness the power of being stuck and help them get unstuck. Finding ways to get unstuck is often difficult, but it is doable, especially when you use found pilots as guideposts along the way, as Ivy U's task force did. Dan Murphy from Murphy Development and Riverton's Lucas Halvorson led very different kinds of companies, but both discovered they could tap into the experience of their employees to make needed changes while strengthening important traditions at the heart of their companies' identities.

We believe that organizational culture is the wellspring of both continuity and change. To make change stick, work with the culture you have, locate found pilots, and use them as the building blocks of cultural change.[14] Listening in will enable you to discover people, places, and projects where the future already lives—where people are trying on new ways of working in positively deviant ways. Each by itself may be small, but together they can turn strategy into action quickly.

CHAPTER 5

Sweeping People In

ALL THE UN-IGNORABLE MOMENTS and found pilots in the world will not create organization-wide change unless you can broaden the effort to include more people than were directly involved in those moments or are engaged in the found pilots. You need a preponderance of people for the change initiative to take on its own momentum, and to move beyond the confines of the offices and labs where it began. And you need the right kind of people—those who can influence others and can create and lead efforts of their own.

But as we've already noted, you cannot compel people to join up. You have to *sweep* people into the action, show them why it's important, make them want to join. For that, you need to put together a coalition of committed individuals who can come together, mobilize other people's energy to the cause, and ensure that supports are put in place to keep the momentum going. The coalition need not be large—some include only a few people—but it needs certain components and practices to be successful, as we'll see.

THE VOLZ FAMILY ENTERPRISE: A FAMILY COALITION

A coalition for sweeping people in can serve many purposes in many different types of organizations. Coalitions in a global enterprise like Quire can identify and spread new growth practices within and across business units. Coalitions can be effective, too, in other kinds of businesses, including family-owned companies, to help diverse factions of a family work together as they face the frictions that arise when a family business reexamines its governance practices.

Meet Volz Family Enterprise, whose story demonstrates the importance of two key components in creating a strong coalition. First, you need a person (or persons) with enough authority to provide cover for others to work in new ways. Second, you need one or more "skeptical friends" who will raise questions that others won't.

The Volz Family Enterprise comprises several operating companies as well as a family foundation, and the parent entity has extensive real estate investments and other liquid assets. Roy Volz, the ninety-year-old paterfamilias, is the only family member who has actually run any of the family's operating businesses, although family members of the first, second, and third generations hold interests within and across multiple family holdings.

The assets of the enterprise are held in a trust managed by the Volz family office. Three trustees run the family office and make all investment decisions for the family portfolio, valued at around $800 million. None of the trustees is a family member. The enterprise also has a board of directors with oversight responsibility for the family office.

The job of the family office trustees is not an easy one. They are legally obligated to serve the varying interests of the beneficiaries, a large and diverse group of people with different concerns and wishes, but have to work with a structure in which the assets are invested for the group as a whole. This structure worked for the first generation because Roy chose the trustees and called the shots about what he wanted them to do with the assets.

When we began working with the family, however, three generations were involved in the enterprise—six siblings in the second generation and twenty-five in the third—so decision-making had become much trickier and more complicated given all the different interests represented. Although family members recognized that the structure wasn't working anymore, they couldn't agree on whether a different structure would make it easier to manage the assets and engage the family in the enterprise. Each faction was worried about losing control if things changed.

An opportunity for change arose when one of the trustees stepped down. A search firm was engaged to find a replacement and, within a few weeks, reported to the board that it had reached an impasse. Qualified candidates were reluctant to consider the job. They all asked the same questions: What is the family looking for in the next trustee? How will the family provide me with guidance about members' collective interests? The candidates were knowledgeable and experienced enough to know that being one of three trustees in a complicated family enterprise meant significant managerial and legal responsibilities, as well as risks. None of the candidates wanted to take on the responsibility without a clear understanding of how decisions would be made—and by whom—in the family. Without a decision-making structure in place, the new trustee might be set up to fail.

Family members asked us to help them answer a question: What do we want for the future? As we conducted interviews, a great deal of mistrust among the siblings of the second generation surfaced and those bad feelings had been passed on to their kids. Some members of the second generation wanted to break up the enterprise so that its value could be distributed. A few members of the third generation did not share the ill will and believed the enterprise should be kept together. They wanted something—beyond wealth—to share with their children. They recognized that leadership and collaboration were needed to accomplish that goal.

These third-generation family members needed some kind of mechanism to give them a base to work from, but the only formal entity in place was the Volz Family Unity Committee, which consisted of two members of the third generation. Its sole responsibility was to plan family reunions. It didn't have much authority or influence, but it was a place to start.

master at using influence in this way; much of his strategy for revising Six Sigma was based on this skill.

———————

WHILE USING YOUR INFLUENCE to mobilize the energy of people who already support your initiative is essential, it's also important to tap into the energy and influence of those who are *not* aligned with you and may actively oppose your ideas. Some influential stakeholders, like Norbert Ball at Quire and Dr. Piersen at University Hospital, may not necessarily be antagonistic. They just have a different set of expectations, and often a different set of interests, about how people should interact with each other and about the obligations each has to others. Their views of the organization's culture, "the way we do things around here," are as natural to them as yours are to you.

It can be tempting to try to ignore the opposition, work around it, or "take it on" in an assertive or aggressive way. These approaches rarely work in the long run. This is where the skeptical friends on your coalition can play an important role. Members of the opposition are not, in most cases, individuals acting on their own. They are members of a network of people who share similar ways of thinking and have similar interests. If you don't know who the influential stakeholders in the opposition are, ask your skeptical friends to help you identify them and help you understand their interests and *why* they believe what they believe. If you respond with genuine interest to the insights of your skeptical friends, they are likely to come up with useful ideas about how to address the concerns of the opposition and find areas of mutual agreement and shared interest.

It's easy to see why so many leaders want to crush the opposition or starve it out. Opposition poses a threat and can drain time and attention from important pursuits, and simply eliminating it may seem useful. But listening in to those who disagree with you improves your understanding of their logic and interests and the groups they are members of. Engaging the opposition is a useful way to increase the social capital you need to spread and sustain new cultural practices. Whether they're for or against you, it pays to identify individuals who influence others.

Beyond your coalition members and the opposition, you need to try and sweep influencers into your efforts. They are the people who supply information to others, for example, about which new initiatives they should pay attention to and support, and which can be ignored, at least for a while. Influencers can help you expand your network in order to mobilize people's energies and align them in the direction you want the organization to move.

Organizational networks usually take the shape of clusters of closely knit groups of people who communicate with each other regularly.[3] There are bound to be many closely knit groups inside your organization, formed around shared interests, roles, or functions. Some people are members of multiple groups. For example, a person in your organization who is a member of an affinity group like La Raza, which focuses on improving opportunities for Hispanic Americans, may also belong to a closely knit group of people who are IT middle managers.

Those who maintain memberships in multiple groups are often called boundary spanners.[4] An influencer who is a boundary spanner brings to each group the perspectives and experience of the other. These people can serve as conduits through which new practices spread from one group, function, department, or business unit to another. They are particularly important in the process of sweeping people in, especially with members of the opposition. Chances are good that boundary spanners have relationships with those who are aligned with, as well as with those who oppose, what you are trying to accomplish.

WHENEVER POSSIBLE, work with boundary spanners to connect groups that contain found pilots. If both groups are working on found pilots, an influential boundary spanner can help connect them. Together they can create a more complete picture of the practices you need to spread. At Quire, many of the opportunities discovered using Six Sigma for Growth came about when one business unit made a connection with what another unit was working on. Jill Norris and Scott James were the first. Recall that Norris and James worked in different business units at Quire and belonged to different organizational networks. Coalition members who spanned those two networks realized that together Norris and James could generate new knowledge management products and services that neither could do on their own.

USING ORGANIZATIONAL NETWORK mapping tools—to determine who's connected to whom and who influences whom—can facilitate sweeping people in by helping you identify the influencers in your organization. Organizational network maps identify tacit relationships among people and make it easier to see the informal communication pathways that news and information follow as they travel through the organization, often at lightning speed.[5]

At University Hospital, we worked with Davidian and Crowley to create a network map of the regularly scheduled meetings at UH, identifying who attended each one. By analyzing the UH networks to identify influencers, Dr. Green identified a few people who regularly participated in many important meetings at UH. This meant they were likely to be members of multiple tightly knit clusters, and some of them likely to be boundary spanners. It only took a little more work to learn which of these influencers had interests aligned with Putting Patients First. Working with them helped Dr. Green and his team spread their team-based approach more broadly and more quickly across the hospital.

NETWORK ANALYSIS is a useful tool for identifying powerful stakeholders who influence others. It does not, however, lay out the underlying, often tacit, "rules" for interaction—the cultural agreements that create coherence within a closely knit group. A savvy leader can use existing social networks to identify those who are influencing others and then use methods like participant observation and shadowing to understand tacit cultural agreements about how work gets done and make them explicit. But first, it's useful to explore how influence works.[6]

Robert Cialdini, in his well-known book *Influence: The Psychology of Persuasion*, articulated six principles of influence that are broadly shared within and across Anglo-European cultures:

- *Reciprocity.* We feel obligated "to repay, in kind, what another person has provided us."
- *Commitment and consistency.* Once we have made a commitment, "we will encounter personal and interpersonal pressure to behave consistently with that commitment. These pressures will cause us to respond in ways that justify our earlier decision."
- *Social proof.* "One means we use to determine what is correct is to find out what other people think is correct." If we want to confirm, for example, that an orthopedic surgeon is an expert in knee replacement surgery, we are likely to talk with others about their experience of that surgeon.
- *Liking.* "We prefer to say yes to requests of someone we know and like."
- *Authority.* We feel a strong sense of duty to authority; and because obedience to authority is often rewarding, it is easy to comply with that authority.
- *Scarcity.* "Opportunities seem more valuable when their availability is limited."

Cialdini examines these six principles of influence from an interpersonal psychological perspective—discussing how we use them to influence each other. He emphasizes that we are trained to respond to cues in ways that he describes as "fixed action patterns."[7]

Where do these principles—and the demands for certain kinds of responses, or Cialdini's "fixed action patterns"—come from? As it turns out, they may not be determined as much by individuals as they are by groups of people who agree, often over long periods of time, about how their members will interact with each other. They are culturally based.

Let's look at reciprocity. Many twentieth-century studies of reciprocity build on the work of French sociologist Marcel Mauss, whose book, *The Gift,* offered a counterargument to early-twentieth-century economic theory.[8] The accepted theory at that time posited that the economics of exchange was an interaction that individuals conducted with each other in rational ways for purely utilitarian purposes: I want something from you, so I give you something in order to get it.

Mauss's work showed that economic exchanges are much more complex than that. Drawing on earlier anthropological fieldwork studies of cultural groups from around the world, he demonstrated that the focus on individuals acting in a rational utilitarian manner in an economic exchange told only part of the story. When we enter an exchange, we carry with us a set of obligations that derive from the cultural agreements we make with others in the groups of which we are members. In other words, individuals act as members of cultural groups, and those groups have rules for interaction that include, for example, an obligation to reciprocate after receiving a gift. Influence works as a way to carry out social obligations, not simply as a utilitarian exchange.

The gift is often as much about maintaining a relationship and social solidarity as it is about the utility of the exchange.

Why is this important? It seems so obvious. *Of course* we reciprocate when someone gives us a gift. *Of course* we are more likely to say yes to someone we like. *Of course* things are more valuable when they are in short supply. That's just the way the world works. But actually it's not—these "principles" are no more (or less) than a set of agreements we've made with one another that create expectations about ways in which we fulfill social obligations. You could say that influence principles are useful because most of us have agreed to them—not because they are the "natural" way to do things. And if we make cultural agreements (and then feel obligated to carry them out), we can also unmake them and create different agreements. We learned this when working with the Hmong, as our relationships with members of the community changed from ethnographers to acquaintances to long-term friends, all with different sets of expectations, obligations, exchanges, and gifts.

So, when working to expand your network and sweep people in to the cultural shift you are leading, remember that influence principles, such as reciprocity, are based on social obligations that underlie and shape the exchanges we have with each other. They are not the only way to do things. It is possible to create new agreements about how work gets done, and about how we interact with each other to get work done. But that does not mean it's easy to change the current cultural agreements. Individual members of all cultural groups consider choices for action based on a repertoire of exchange rules that are for the most part tacit—developed over time, handed down from one generation to the next, and taught as "the natural way to do things."

Sets of tacit expectations and rules for interaction—both internally and externally—are the cultural lifeblood of any organization. In order to build social capital and make room for new practices, it helps to first understand the current social rules for interaction and influence that operate inside your organization. Only then can you identify new ways of working that stretch the current culture without being rejected by it. And it's a safe bet to act on the assumption that individuals are not just lone actors—we are always members of groups with sets of shared beliefs, and our behavior is never truly all of our own making. As Margaret Mead is reported to have said, "Remember you are unique. Just like everybody else."

STRENGTHENING SUPPORTS TO SUSTAIN NEW CULTURAL PRACTICES

Now we come to the second aspect of the leadership task of sweeping people in: finding and strengthening the supports that will help shape and sustain the behaviors you've discovered through working with found pilots. At University Hospital, for example, Dr. Green helped sustain the team-based practices of his operating room team by deploying a number of supports: checklists, a system for tracking local performance against national quality and patient safety measures, and an engaged, supportive, motivating leadership style.

It works best to find supports that connect with the existing culture while encouraging positively deviant changes to it. Quire had a history of aggressive direct sales with their customer base. But when Gus and his team invited Quire's customers to the data security workshop, the Six Sigma for Growth team stipulated there would be no selling of Quire offerings during the meeting. The sales force was furious, but their business unit president went along with the experiment. Six Sigma for Growth tools and methods were familiar enough to Quire's culture to make it possible to experiment with a different approach to sales in the workshop. Fortunately, the coalition's indirect marketing approach resulted in many millions of dollars of sales for Quire—but it was risky. The tools and methods of Six Sigma provided the kind of support that made it a smart risk.

Often the supports you need are already in place, and they just need to be adapted to your needs. Jeanne Rice, the director of the InSight Institute, a research center for eye surgery, faced a major challenge. Grant-giving institutions, such as the National Institutes of Health (NIH), were increasing the grants awarded to team-based, interdisciplinary research, and decreasing the number and amount of grants to individual researchers. Rice had made the business case to her colleagues that it was necessary to shift InSight's culture of research from individual projects by institute scientists to a team-based approach. Not surprisingly, individual researchers balked.

To sweep them in, Rice needed to find ways to support team-based behavior. She realized InSight had a financial incentive already in place that could be adapted to encourage more teams of researchers to apply for grants. InSight had been charging teams a fee to cover administrative costs and deducting it from their grants, which had been a bone of contention between researchers and administration for some time. Rice announced that the administrative fee would be reduced by 50 percent for researchers who proposed interdisciplinary team-based projects. The amount was significant enough that it stimulated researchers to go after grants for team-based research, and it made the institute more attractive to the kind of talent they were trying to attract that would strengthen further interdisciplinary team-based research. The culture began to shift from individual to interdisciplinary initiatives.

Finding and strengthening existing supports that fit with the cultural shift you're trying to make has a number of advantages. First, they are usually much less expensive than putting money into new support systems, which often require heavy up-front investment. And cultural shifts often occur when resources are scarce, when it's not viable (or even possible) to hire new people or make financial investments in new systems.

Investing in new support systems can be costly in other ways as well. The opportunity cost incurred by those who are asked to introduce and manage them is high. In addition, the systems often run counter to existing cultural agreements for how work gets done, as they are intended to force new ways of working. Without connecting them, however, to the practices you want to see in action—the everyday behaviors and new ways of working on the ground that you need to make a cultural shift—new and unfamiliar support systems can backfire.

Existing support systems, on the other hand, are known entities. Any resistance to them has already faded. Strengthening an existing system that helps support new practices can make them easier to adopt. There are almost always existing work processes, accountability and decision-making systems, information-sharing efforts, reward systems, and communication systems that can be used, adapted, repurposed, or reconfigured to support new ways of working. Finding and strengthening supports already in place can help ensure new resources get focused in the best way.

Rockledge Insurance is a company that strengthened existing supports after learning more about the behaviors it wanted to encourage. The company was trying to speed up its claims process by enabling teams in the field to make decisions at the damage site. This would render the claims process much more efficient, reduce payment time by up to three weeks, and make customers a lot happier.

Speeding up the process required making changes in the way things had been done for years. Claims adjustors were used to assessing damage on the site of a potential claim—such as after a hurricane—filling out standard forms and sending them to the central office. There, within three or four weeks, the claims would be processed, and payment, in the form of a paper check, would be sent to the insured.

As you can anticipate by now, we suggested they step back and ask the question, "Where is the future you're trying to create already showing up?" People in the central office knew that most claims adjustors were using computers at their field offices to communicate with the central office and that some of them had even created their own electronic forms to make the process faster and more efficient. They sent representatives out to shadow some of these tech-savvy claims adjustors to see if they could learn from them about how to change the process. They discovered that most claims adjustors were eager to improve the process in ways that benefited customers, the company, and themselves.

While the field research was under way, the central claims office also conducted its own research. Claims data for the preceding five years revealed that only 20 percent of the claims needed investigation by the central office while 80 percent could be processed without review. This convinced claims central leadership that the process could, and should, be changed.

To sweep people in to the behaviors of the tech-savvy adjustors, claims central needed to provide supports that would turn the new ways of working into sustainable, everyday practices. So claims central took action. Building on the electronic forms that some adjustors in the field had already created, it supplied adjustors with digital tablets they could use in the field. A program was created that would identify claims that needed further investigation and review and screen out the 80 percent that could be processed swiftly. Claims central also made adjustments to the existing training program now led by the tech-savvy claims adjustors, so that field people were able to learn from their colleagues.

As a result, adjustors could communicate with claims central from the field and in most cases make payments on the spot.

They have adopted the new way of working with the ongoing help of strong support systems—computers, easy-to-use applications designed by adjustors, and training. The system works better for everyone.

———————

SOMETIMES THE BEST WAY to strengthen existing support structures is to propose an alternative that puts both the valuable and the unhelpful parts of the existing structure into relief. Many of the tacit assumptions and agreements that motivated the creation of the current structure can then come to the fore, and decisions can be made about what to keep and what to change.

The comparison between current and alternative support structures can serve as a springboard to a deeper understanding of why those supports were created in the first place: What are we trying to accomplish? What are the things that matter most? What will hold us together when the going gets rough?

Questions like these were at the heart of the issue facing Vargas & Co., a family business based in southern California. Its founder, Emilio Vargas, had developed five different businesses in the entertainment industry. Emilio and his wife, Isabel, had always felt blessed that they had five children, four boys and a girl, all of whom entered the family's businesses. Emilio's first business was a record label, Vargas World Music. Now well-known as a Latin music label, its success had enabled Emilio to branch out to concert promotions, a sound and lighting company, a couple of performance theaters, and a public relations business.

When Emilio Vargas retired, he stipulated that each of his five children would run one business, but all five would have an ownership stake in the five businesses that made up the family enterprise. His goal was to keep the second generation together after he was no longer there. Emilio's oldest son, Angel, had come up working in the recording business. As the oldest male, he was being groomed to take over the jewel in the family crown, Vargas World Music. The three middle children, now adults with children in their early twenties, ran the concert promotion business, the sound and lighting company, and the performance theaters. For the past seven years Mercedes, the youngest and Emilio's only daughter, had been CEO of the public relations firm her father had established in Dallas, Texas. She had met her husband there, and they had two small children.

Emilio's plan worked well for some time, but a few years after Vargas Senior died, the three middle sons decided they wanted more autonomy and control over the businesses each led. Angel and Mercedes didn't see the need to change the governance structure. They believed their father had made the right decision, and it had worked well. It had kept them united as a family, and that was, they said, what mattered most in the end.

The five siblings were at an impasse. They were stuck. At the same time, some of their own children were asking to work in the family businesses, specifically Vargas World Music. Suddenly everything became more complicated. The five siblings in the second generation had to figure out what they were going to do now that their children were ready to become part of the family's businesses. How connected did they need to be? It was easy to see that their children could enter the business that each led—but what about working across businesses? And what would that mean when their children had children? Angel had just become a grandparent the previous year.

They knew that if they could not address the differences within their own generation, planning for the next generation would be impossible. The family enterprise could be torn apart. They needed to figure out how to deal with the tension between the desire for greater individual autonomy and the belief that their father's focus on interdependence was the best way to ensure family and business continuity.

When we first met with the five siblings, it became clear they had not spent much time working together on the combined family enterprise since their father had passed away four years earlier. When they did get together, it was mostly for family occasions, and their conversations focused on the kids and how they were doing. Their modus operandi: "Don't ask me anything about my business, and I won't ask you anything about yours." Although some wanted greater autonomy and control over the businesses they ran, none actually knew the market value of the individual businesses. This was going to be, as it usually is, a business problem as well as a family problem.

Noting the family tension in our first meeting, we recommended that we all work together to explore what it would mean to create greater autonomy as an alternative to the current governance structure. We knew from prior experience that there are many issues at play inside a family's decision to create a set of autonomous businesses versus retaining an interdependent ownership structure, and only some of them had to do with money. Family businesses are usually as much about the family as they are about the business, and a viable governance structure has to address the needs of both.

We focused on the businesses by first calibrating the value of each. It was the first time they had ever made this important calculation, and the process opened up conversations about what a business might sell for. It built a shared foundation among the five siblings to think about what it would mean if each had control over a business and owned it exclusively. This was eye-opening. In some cases the value of the operating company was eclipsed by the real estate it occupied. For others, the operating company's growth functioned like a magnet, drawing outside parties interested in making a market for it.

As they worked together to understand the possibilities and implications of separating the equity, the siblings began to see that the challenge they faced was more complex than they had assumed. For example, the sound and lighting business actually lost money but sat on land that had been purchased decades ago, which could be repurposed for greater returns. Yet the brother who ran this business was so deeply attached to it, that repurposing it would be like "cutting off my arm." On the other hand, Vargas World Music, run by the oldest, Angel, was widely known. Wherever the family went, people would ask about the record business, remark on its longevity, and express admiration for the family. This business made money but was also an icon, and because it was run by the oldest, the younger family members actually wanted in more. Angel had become the Vargas family patriarch after Emilio's death.

Working with the siblings to understand the economics of each business was critical to illuminating their different perspectives regarding autonomy. It enabled conversations that were both grounded and broadening. What really mattered to them? What was the nature of their relationships, both economic and familial? Was their father a domineering autocrat, ruling from the grave, or a prescient wise man recognizing that his children would come to value the skills each brought to the enterprise as a whole, making the whole greater than the sum of its parts?

Through our work together, the five siblings came to the collective realization that, while greater autonomy was desirable, it would be foolish to minimize the value the family name provided to each of the businesses, to them personally, and to the next generation to join the family enterprise.

We recommended a hybrid solution that balanced the need for autonomy with the value of family interdependence. The operating companies would remain separate, but they would create a governance structure for the entire family enterprise. The siblings would have to make major capital decisions, such as the purchase or sale of a business, together. Decisions would not need to be unanimous, but they worked to specify rules by which they could run the businesses both independently and together. The governance, structural, and procedural recommendations were well received. As one of the brothers noted after they had all agreed to implement the recommendations,

"By exploring an alternative to the structure our dad had put in place, you helped us come to know our own mind."

BAKE WITH THE FLOUR YOU HAVE

Don't take on the task of sweeping people in by yourself. Rely on your coalition members to help you. They will work with you to sweep people in to spread and support the work of your found pilots. Engaging key stakeholders and working with influencers—especially boundary spanners and members of the opposition—is the fastest and most effective way to spread new ideas through tried-and-true informal communication channels.

As new ways of working spread through the organization, they need support. Try to strengthen the support systems already in place. As the old folk saying goes, "Bake with the flour you have." Strengthening familiar support systems, sometimes by exploring alternatives, just as the Vargas siblings did, can help people make choices needed to build a bridge from current to new ways of getting work done—choices that reinforce the value of existing traditions while making room for needed change.

Building social capital, engaging coalitions, and strengthening existing support structures are critical to creating a sustainable cultural shift. There is, however, no substitute for leadership. Leading in times of continuous change takes an additional set of skills that many of us find counterintuitive at first. But as Ken Patterson discovers in the next chapter, the most difficult challenge you face may be getting out of your own way.

CHAPTER 6

The Case of a Leader
Who Finds a
New Kind of Power

AMY MARSHFIELD CALLED ME LATE one December afternoon, just as I was getting ready to leave the office. I'd
worked with Amy when she was president of a small
liberal arts college, and remembered her as calm and cool, always maintaining a level head and having the ability to see a
situation from many sides. Her voice on the phone, however,
conveyed tension and concern. We took a couple of minutes to
catch up, with Amy reminding me that she was now a member
of the board of trustees of Moncrieff University, a midsize school
in the Northeast. Like many academic institutions, Moncrieff
had been going through difficult times: enrollment and endow-
ment were both down and financial concerns were mounting.

Amy then got to the reason for the call: "Barry, we're having some issues with our president. He's not even a year into his tenure and he's rubbed more than a few people the wrong way."

"I see. Is it a matter of strategic direction? Academics? Personality?"

"Probably all three. That's what I need to discuss with you."

We talked a bit more. Amy reminded me that nine months earlier, Moncrieff's board had made a bold move, hiring a new president from outside the world of academia—Kenneth Patterson, an internationally known figure in the world of finance.

"What brought him to Moncrieff?" I asked.

"He wanted a different kind of challenge," Amy replied. "He had always loved academia, and also had a lot of management and board experience. He liked the idea of working with an institution that had great potential and where he thought he could really make a difference."

The move surprised faculty and staff at Moncrieff—their presidents had always been academics—but this kind of hire was not out of step with what was going on at other universities, large and small, as they struggled to navigate the roiling waters of change in higher education. Moncrieff needed someone who could help the university recover from the economic collapse of 2008, and revitalize its finances amid tight times. Hiring Patterson was bold but risky.

Unfortunately, things had not gone as well as the board had hoped.

"To be blunt," Amy said. "Not everyone's a fan." She sighed. "I'm afraid we're in a bit of a mess and I don't see the way out."

"Has anybody on the board given Patterson feedback about the transition and his management style?"

"No, I guess we haven't been that direct. And I should know that this is what you would counsel us to do."

I had advised many boards over the years and we agreed to get together the following day to see if I could be of assistance in working with the new president.

THE MONCRIEFF CAMPUS looked like many other college campuses of its kind. The quad, the bustling students, the red brick classroom buildings and dorms, the president's mansion, which seemed a little the worse for wear.

I met Amy in a conference room in the admissions building and she introduced me to board chairman Owen Roth, a Moncrieff alum and self-made success in the software business. Roth was one of Patterson's first and most ardent supporters, but now, Amy had told me, he was feeling some buyer's remorse, as were other trustees. After introductions and a few pleasantries, Roth plunged into the issue. "It's all China's fault," he said, chuckling without any real sparkle of humor. Amy smiled faintly. I waited and listened carefully as a good ethnographer would.

Roth continued. "Long before Patterson came on board, we had embarked on a highly ambitious development project. The Moncrieff Center for Innovation, based in China, partnering with a new educational institution in Shenzhen. The idea is to create a curriculum and incubate research and development activities that focus on innovation, creative thinking, problem solving, and—here's the intriguing twist—all linked to issues of manufacturing and supply chain."

Shenzhen, of course, is the major manufacturing center in southern China, source of many of the world's electronic components and consumer goods, and a key node on the global supply chain. I had traveled there a few times myself and know how quickly it has grown into an industrial powerhouse for China.

"It's Moncrieff's first overseas venture outside of study abroad programs," Amy added. "And the entire university is excited about it."

"But President Patterson is not?"

"No, no—quite the opposite," said Roth. "Ken took the idea and ran with it. That's the problem. He more than ran with it. He ran away with it."

This was a bit unusual. In my experience working with executives in all kinds of organizations, an incoming leader was more likely to ditch the projects of the predecessor. I was happy to hear that Patterson had not followed that pattern, because it can be very difficult for the people who developed the plan and still support it.

"Yes," Amy said. "Ken got so enthusiastic about the potential of the China project to help us financially that he threw his arms around it." At his first board meeting, Patterson had convincingly argued that in the current market interdisciplinary studies could attract grant money and might also bring in additional support, even investment, from the Chinese government. Roth agreed with the plan in theory, and the board gave its blessing to continue.

Then the ambitious Dr. Patterson, I learned, had unilaterally decided that the Center for Innovation, instead of being a standalone facility, would be the centerpiece of a new, interdisciplinary, global campus. To realize his vision, Patterson had set off on a private road show, traveling across the country and making more than one trip to China, identifying and meeting with potential partners and investors, drumming up interest and pledges of capital support.

"Wait a minute," I said. "Let me get this straight. Patterson didn't consult the board about his activities?"

"No. He might have mentioned that he was having some meetings about the center, but certainly did not ask for our advice or approval," Roth said. "Nor did he check in with the faculty or the administration. During his first few months on campus, Ken was rarely in his office. Even his chief of staff didn't always know where to find him. And our chief financial officer is in shock!"

"He's pretty good about texting, though," Amy admitted. "That's more his style."

Amy added more details. She had received numerous calls and emails from several of the deans she had gotten close to on campus, especially those who had been involved in developing the China project. They wanted to know what was going on with the program, what Patterson was up to, and what his future role would be.

Money was a particularly sensitive issue. Budgets had been tight at Moncrieff throughout the recession, and even though the pressure had been easing up, the university stayed its conservative fiscal course. Several departments had been waiting for increased allocations for years and were still waiting. Much needed faculty hires had been postponed. The construction of a new science building had been put on hold. Now Patterson seemed ready to devote scarce resources to the China project without discussing finances with the deans and faculty leaders. And to make matters worse, the new president was out gallivanting around the globe, spending God knows how much money on travel, presentations, and entertaining. I could see that this approach would not go over well.

"I think it's fair to say that most of the faculty members, many of the deans, and not a few board members are less than pleased," Roth said. "We're facing some fundamental issues right now. We have to address our finances while improving academic quality—our rankings have been slipping—and still going forward with new initiatives, particularly the China project. For all of that, we need leadership. And I don't think we're getting exactly the kind of leadership we need from Ken. Some of the trustees who were skeptical about hiring him from the start are saying I told you so. I personally think it's too soon to pass judgment. But, there is no question the natives are getting restless. If I may use that term . . ."

"You can't," Amy said. "Although it's accurate. And confidentially, I have even heard rumors that the university provost, Renee Carleton, is planning to resign."

Carleton, as provost and thus the chief academic officer of the university, had long been a defender of the school's liberal arts mission, and she felt it was now under siege—as were the liberal arts at many institutions like Moncrieff. A scholar of European social history, Carleton had been resisting pressure to cut faculty positions in the humanities and social sciences, and she saw the new investment in China as a slap in the face, not because of the initiative itself but because of the decision making connected with it. Losing her would be a serious blow to Moncrieff and its reputation.

"That's not the only rumor flying around," Owen added. "I'm also hearing that Ken could be whacked with a vote of no confidence from the faculty. Largely because of his getting out in front of everybody on the China project. This could turn out to be one of those derailed presidencies."

That sounded precipitous and unlikely so early in Patterson's reign. Still, these kinds of incidents were becoming increasingly common on campuses around the country. University presidents were regularly challenged by their colleagues, voted down by faculties, questioned by their boards—an indication of just how tense and uncertain conditions were in the world of higher education.[1]

"I don't know if Ken has heard any of these rumors," Owen said. "Nor am I sure we should tell him. They're not confirmed, after all. Campuses are always rife with tales and half-truths."

"Well, I do know that Ken will be speaking at tomorrow's meeting of the council of deans to update them about progress on the Shenzhen campus," Amy added. "So, maybe he has heard the rumblings and is trying to respond."

Maybe. I had a great desire to be a fly on the wall at that meeting, not only to hear what Patterson might say but to observe his interaction with the deans. A bit of listening in.

Owen looked to me. "What do you think, Barry?"

"I would advocate strongly for letting him know what's going on. You don't want him to be blindsided," I said. "And I think there is way too much back-channel communication going on here to be helpful in building a strong relationship between the board and the new president."

"Otherwise, let's see how the meeting with the deans plays out. Depending on what happens, you can decide what and how much to tell him about what you're hearing."

"I have a dinner with him that evening," Owen said. "A glass of wine or two could help bring out the story."

———————

WE PARTED, and I spent the better part of the afternoon doing research on Moncreiff's hyperactive leader. Kenneth Patterson, 59, had been raised in the Midwest, was the first member of his family to go to college, earned his PhD in international finance, then promptly built a sizable fortune running a hedge fund. He used the proceeds to get into venture capital, did some consulting, wrote a book or two, became a fixture on the lecture circuit (TED talk, of course), picked up a couple of honorary degrees, served on several boards of directors, traveled all over the world, and seemed to have read every book written in English, as well as in the four other languages he spoke. Almost always the smartest person in the room, except (perhaps) for the time he spent with his buddies Bill Clinton, Warren Buffett, and Daniel Kahneman. He'd spent his recent years at the very top of the intellectual, financial, and social food chain, and I began to wonder if he, like some others in his position, had forgotten how to play nicely with others.

―――――――

A FEW DAYS LATER, I got a call from Owen Roth. The meeting with the deans had not gone well. Patterson had taken the stage and made yet another bold announcement. He had forged a partnership, he proclaimed, with one of the nation's leading software companies (whose founder was, of course, a personal friend of his), and the firm had agreed to finance a significant amount of the China campus's infrastructure. "This is an enormous win!" Patterson had crowed. "We'll draw students from every corner of the earth. We'll create jobs. Put a spotlight on innovation. Push the name of Moncrieff University in the headlines and on Twitter feeds around the world!"

Patterson was on a high. When he finished, he looked out at the deans, as if expecting a round of applause or perhaps a coronation. Instead, he was greeted with silence and stony faces. Patterson, never one to be intimidated, asked for questions or comments.

There were many. What role do you see for the faculty and staff in further development of plans for the center? What is your vision for Moncrieff—as a sort of high-end trade school? What kind of relationships are proper with corporate partners?

"How did he handle the questions?" I asked.

"He kept cool at first. But then he turned defensive. Then he got angry and finally sanctimonious. He started lecturing the deans—it's never wise to lecture the lecturers—about how they lacked vision and were exhibiting classic resistance to change behaviors, and that their benighted thinking and intransigence was what put Moncrieff in such a hole in the first place."

"Wow. Sounds like he lost it."

"For sure he lost it. And then came the kicker."

"What was that?"

"The provost, Renee Carleton—the one we heard rumors about—stood up, marched to the front of the room, jumped up to Ken, and announced her resignation."

"Wow again."

"Even Ken could see that things were getting out of control. He tried to make light of it, as if the provost were joking. But then she made a passionate speech about how her resignation was more than a personal choice: it was a statement of principle, about how the president was leading. Or not leading. And, she said, her views represented those of most of the faculty. With that, she promptly made her exit, leaving Ken with an even more impassioned crowd to deal with."

Then, just as the meeting was threatening to get really out of hand, the dean of the school of engineering, Francis Randolph, rose from his chair and strolled calmly to the front of the room. He waved his hand as if stirring the air and the room instantly quieted. Randolph, a soft-spoken gentleman in his mid-sixties, turned to Patterson and smiled in a courtly fashion.

"President Patterson," he said. "I'd like to ask you a question if I may."

Patterson appreciated how Randolph had calmed the tone of the discussion. "Of course," he said, teeth clenched. "Why not?"

"Thank you," Randolph said. "It's a rather basic question. What do you consider to be the single most distinctive and distinguishing characteristic of Moncrieff University? Its essential nature. Its true soul."

The question caught Patterson by surprise. He paused. He looked blank. The side conversations among the audience members abruptly stopped. Patterson cleared his throat. Everyone was listening carefully, craning forward, waiting for his answer.

"Well, I guess," Patterson said, obviously playing for time, sensing that this question was of great importance but that he really did not have the "right" answer or much of an answer at all. "Well, ah, I would have to say, I guess, being honest, that, ah, well . . ." and then he seemed to shed his caution and indecision. "I would have to say that we don't have a particularly distinctive characteristic. Except, perhaps, for fiscal distress. But that is hardly distinguishing." He almost laughed, as if trying to make a joke, but realized as the air escaped his lungs that he was headed in the wrong direction and managed to convert the near laugh into a meaningless guttural gulp.

Shocked silence. *Patterson doesn't even think Moncrieff has a distinctive characteristic except fiscal distress? No essential nature? No soul?*

"I see," Dr. Randolph said, "thank you." He sat down again. Somehow, Randolph's presence and the nature of his question had galvanized the feeling in the room. *The guy cares for nothing but money. The stereotype holds true.* Owen paused, as if recounting anything further about that evening was beyond him at the moment.

"What about the no-confidence vote?" I asked.

"That's pretty much in the hands of Alicia Chang, dean of arts and sciences. Although the chair of the faculty senate technically calls the vote, Alicia has a lot of influence on the faculty and on whether a vote of no confidence would even be considered. In any case, the earliest it could happen would be in about two weeks, after she gets back to campus."

"Then Dr. Patterson has some time to make amends."

"Yes, if he's inclined to. And knows how." Owen paused. "Listen, Barry, at dinner I mentioned you and your work to Ken. He wasn't initially interested. Said he's not a fan of consultants and advisers and coaches. But I suggested to him that the board, and its chair, felt otherwise. The long and the short of it is he's agreed to meet with you."

I knew that I could only be of use to Patterson (and to Moncrieff) if he genuinely wanted to improve the situation. That remained to be seen.

PATTERSON, UNSURPRISINGLY, did not call me. A week went by. I waited. Then I got a call that I thought might be Patterson (judging by the area code), but it was Owen Roth. He sounded dispirited. The board had met the evening before and Patterson had continued in his swashbuckling ways. When it came time for his report, he had leaped up, raced through a PowerPoint update of the China project plans (including the strategic partnership with the software company), and then announced that he was developing a new, twenty-year strategic plan for the university.

"A *twenty-year* plan? Did I hear you right?" I asked.

"Yes. I pointed out to him that we're in year three of a five-year plan and that we had engaged in a major campus-wide process to develop it. And that we would begin development of the next plan a year hence."

"The board knew nothing about this?"

"No. Ken said that he'd had a vision on a flight back from Hong Kong and had just started madly scribbling. He said that the board had to think bigger. Farther out. And, furthermore, that our current five-year plan was too timid. Too so-what. The whole educational system is on the brink of monumental change and this is our chance to become a leader."

"How did that go over?" I asked.

Owen gave me a blow by blow of the rest of the presentation. The trustees probed Ken on his plans and his process. "When had you planned to involve the board? Do you believe in a top-down approach to planning? Did you seek any input from the faculty? Can we really plan twenty years out? How do you characterize the monumental change facing the educational system? What does being a leader mean to you?" Patterson had been chipper and relished the interaction. He believed that a strategic plan had to start with the leader. Consensus wouldn't work for strategy. Of course, he intended to involve the board and the faculty eventually, but only when he felt the plan was far enough along for meaningful input from them. Patterson believed he was appropriately fulfilling his leadership role while effectively managing human resources.

"What about the meeting with the deans and the provost's resignation? Did those issues come up?" I asked.

"Oh yes. That was the first question after Ken had revealed his plans for us over the next two decades."

"How did he respond?"

"It was unfortunate, he said. New leadership often results in changes in other positions. Ho-hum. Change is tough sometimes. Gotta get the right people on the bus. Blah blah blah."

"I see."

"A solo strategic plan. Blasé about Carleton's departure. Then came the pièce de résistance."

"I'm all ears."

"I pressed Ken about Carleton. Was he going to talk with her? Try to bring her back? If not, what about a replacement? Was he planning to conduct a search? When? How?"

I had a very bad feeling that I knew what Patterson's reply had been. I had seen this once before with another university president who was tone deaf to the consequences of his actions.

"Did Ken, by any chance, say that he would assume the position of provost?" I asked, hoping to hear a no.

"Good God, you're prescient or psychic or something," Owen said. "That's exactly what he did. Said he'd be willing to serve as interim provost through next summer. That would give us plenty of time to think about roles and responsibilities. And we'd save some money, too."

Owen and I talked for another twenty minutes or so. Although he had definitely come to the conclusion that Patterson had to change his ways, and at least half the board agreed with him, some of the other trustees saw Patterson's moves as strong leadership. "He's a bit tough, sure, but that's what we need right now. Our last strategic planning process was a disaster anyway, don't you remember? Consensus building is a nightmare and results in lowest-common-denominator bromides. Look, he's already got half the China project funded. It wasn't professional of Carleton to resign in a public meeting. It was grandstanding." On and on it went. The evening had ended long after the appointed hour and the trustees straggled off home or for a nightcap or to catch a plane to their next meeting.

―――――――

THE FOLLOWING EVENING I received a call from Dr. Kenneth Patterson, he of the billion dollars and multiple degrees and twenty-year plan for a new educational institution. Patterson was crisp, self-confident, and perfectly polite. He was also "concerned," as he put it, and had decided to follow his board chair's advice and give me a call.

"Not that I think we have any fundamental operational, structural, or administrative problems we can't overcome," he said. "But I must confess there are some behaviors here at Moncrieff that I find puzzling. I'm really rather stunned that the faculty would even consider a no-confidence vote. And that the board of trustees would have any doubts about the necessity of a long-range plan. It's baffling and frustrating to me. Not what I'm used to at all."

"How do you read the situation?"

"It's obvious. They want me to fail. I'm not a true member of the academic tribe, even though I've got more degrees than the four most senior deans combined. I'm the Wall Street bad guy. The carpetbagger. The suit who thought it would be fun to become a university president. Just a lark. But they, the serious ones, *they* have tenure on the line. Families to feed. Young minds to shape for the good of the world! Academic disciplines to further!"

"Why *were* you interested in this job?"

Perhaps no one had asked Patterson that question before. Or perhaps the timing was right for it to catch him off guard.

"Why indeed," he said and then paused for a moment. When he spoke again, he had lost his sarcastic tone. "Listen, I deeply believe in the importance of education. I strongly believe that our educational system is flawed and in serious need of fresh ideas and new directions. I've been involved in several successful turnarounds in my career. I've stepped into unfamiliar situations, learned fast, and made a difference. I think there are too many people with skills and resources who spend too long on Wall Street or in C-suites in big corporations and don't engage enough with the really important issues like the future of education in this country. That's why I wanted to take on this challenge. But all I see here is resistance to change and a desire to preserve the precious status quo, masquerading as personal dislike for my so-called leadership style."

His passion was undeniable. Here was a man who knew what he wanted, was used to getting what he wanted, was used to convincing, cajoling or—if necessary—vanquishing his adversaries. But in this unaccustomed university environment his way of working was not, in fact, working. If faculty members weren't behind him and the board didn't support him, what then? He did not own this "company." He couldn't fire everyone. He couldn't kick out the trustees. He could leave, but he didn't want to and he would see it as a defeat. He sensed in his gut that something had to change. He just didn't quite know what. Or how.

I said nothing for a moment and then asked a question. "Is that why you're proposing to take on the role of chief academic officer?"

"Precisely. I have to get inside the *materiality* of the work. Be able to influence the stuff that really matters: the curriculum, the approach to teaching, all of that. If I can get some innovation going there, then it will follow elsewhere. The China project is great, but it's far away. It won't necessarily change anything here on the good old Moncrieff quad."

"Do you have any allies in this move?"

"Allies? I have no allies. I'm the enemy, remember? Besides, it's not my job to become best buddies with the faculty and staff. Even if I wanted to, I've been so busy getting out there, doing inconsequential things like raising money and building partnerships with powerful people who can help us, that I've barely had time to finish the book I'm working on, let alone slurp coffee with twelve deans and guzzle sherry with 132 professors. They do drink sherry, don't they?"

He stopped. He snorted in frustration. Then he laughed.

"Wait a minute. I just remembered! Alicia Chang!"

I wasn't sure at first who he was talking about, although I remembered hearing the name. "Alicia Chang?"

"Yes. She's the dean of arts and sciences. I'd totally forgotten about her. She's been away for some time." Turns out Patterson had served on the board of a charitable organization with Chang some years ago. She was a well-respected Moncrieff scientist and faculty leader, who had chaired the biology department before becoming dean. Kenneth liked Alicia, trusted her, and knew she had the respect of some of the other deans and department chairs, and of the faculty as a whole. She was the one who had been missing at the council meeting. Perhaps she would have spoken on his behalf if she had been there.

"Could you reach out to her?" I asked. "Maybe she can give you some clues as to the strange cultural ways here."

"That's entirely possible."

Then I had another thought. It was worth a try. "Perhaps she'd consider stepping in as an interim provost," I suggested. "Given the China project, the twenty-year strategy, the threat of a no-confidence vote, and that book you're writing, perhaps you could take that task off the table."

"That's not a bad idea," Patterson said.

I GUESS IT WAS ACTUALLY a decent idea because Patterson did in fact reach out to Alicia Chang. Not that he told me he was going to do so—I learned all this from him much later, after he and I had developed a much stronger relationship.

Anyway, Patterson caught a bit of luck in that the faculty, distracted by the December holidays, postponed the no-confidence vote once and then once again, and finally put it off until after the New Year, since so many of them would be out of town, out of the office, or otherwise out of pocket. Patterson texted Alicia while she was on her travels (delivering a series of lectures in Beijing), describing the issues to her in two-sentence tidbits, and hinting that he would like her to take on the role of interim provost. He offered to fly to Beijing to meet with her and discuss matters further, but she sensibly suggested that such a move would not improve the optics of the situation—another first-class flight to the already sensitive country of China—and besides, she was returning soon anyway.

With no board meetings scheduled, and everyone more or less distracted by the holidays, Patterson laid low, spending most of his time behind closed doors in his office.

As PATTERSON DESCRIBED to me later, the meeting with Alicia Chang, when it finally happened, was "bracing," "refreshingly candid," and "surprisingly enlightening," and revealed a key bit of information that had previously eluded him. Seems that the faculty's objection to the China project had less to do with

Patterson's manner or his partnerships with beneficent software companies or even his high-mileage globe-trotting, and more to do with his relationship—or lack thereof—with a senior faculty member: Francis C. K. Randolph, dean of the school of engineering, the very person who, at the deans council meeting, had asked what had become known on campus as "the soul question" and who would have a lot to say about when, or if, the no-confidence vote would be called.

Patterson had met Randolph once or twice but had little engagement with him. The first real encounter between them had come at the council meeting, but, despite the reaction Randolph had gotten from the audience, his place in the university's culture had not fully registered with Patterson. Alicia filled him in. Randolph was nothing less than the spiritual leader of Moncrieff University, its secular priest, its cultural sachem. He had been teaching there for thirty-seven years and had held virtually every position of significance, including dean of faculty, department chair (architecture and engineering, although he also held a degree in the classics), and now dean of the engineering school, but had recently announced that he would give up his official positions and cut back on his course load. To those who did not know him well, including President Patterson, it appeared that Frank Randolph was slowly tilting toward retirement. Not so, Alicia said. In fact, quite the opposite. It had long been assumed in faculty circles, although never publicly acknowledged, that Frank would be named leader of the China project. He had the credentials, the gravitas, the international reputation, and the almost universal support of faculty and staff. He had been intimately involved in developing the China plan, but then Patterson came aboard and shut him out. Patterson had never once had a conversation with Randolph about China or anything else of substance, for that matter.

"Randolph is key to whether the no-confidence vote is called," Alicia had told Patterson.

"But the by-laws clearly state that it's the president of the Faculty Senate who calls the vote," he had replied.

"Sure. That's the mechanics of the situation. But everyone listens to Frank. And to me."

Patterson had considered this. "So what do I do? Grovel?"

"No. You go listen to him." She smiled. "After you do, we can talk about the interim provost position."

"I see," Patterson had replied. "Cornered."

———

PERHAPS THAT FEELING of being cornered is why Ken Patterson called me a few days later.

"Barry," he began (calling me by name for the first time), "I wonder if you would be free to join me for an important meeting."

"Glad to if I can. Who with?"

"Dr. Frank Randolph. Engineering guy. Supposedly thinks he's entitled to lead the China project. Also, I'm told, quite influential with the faculty."

"How could I be of help there?"

"Well, you seem to have some understanding of the medieval machinations of this place that I don't, and I thought you might be able to keep me from pissing anybody off, which I seem to do with some regularity."

"That's one of my most finely tuned skills," I said.

"Good," said Patterson. "Tea tomorrow at Randolph's lair."

I MET PATTERSON in the hallway outside Randolph's office. I won't say he was nervous, but he did seem slightly ill at ease.

"I really don't know how to talk with these people," he said to me, sotto voce. "They speak in academic code. I've been out of this world too long. I'm rusty with the language."

"You'll be fine," I said, sensing that he was approaching some kind of tipping point. He couldn't bulldoze any more; he'd learned that much. Now the issues had come down to a single, essential task: getting Randolph on his side. Then perhaps other pieces would fall into place. Patterson liked the clarity and focus of that, far better than trying to bring along a board of trustee volunteers or dealing with a hostile faculty mob.

Randolph welcomed us into his study. It was not the book-lined monastic cell that Patterson seemed to expect. Instead, its shelves were filled with three-dimensional architectural and engineering models. Great classical buildings and modernist masterpieces, bridges and towers and monuments.

"Good God," said Patterson, dashing over to a scale model of a slender, seven-masted bridge. "I've driven over that damned thing a dozen times. Magical!"

I recognized the structure but could not conjure up its name or any details about it.

"The Millau viaduct," Patterson said, as if it were completely obvious. "Cable-stayed. Tallest bridge in the world. Designed by Norman Foster. The British architect."

"Oh right," I said. "Yes. In France. South. Right?"

"A feat of design and engineering," added Frank, nodding benevolently toward me. "*Engineered* by Dr. Michel Virlogeux. At least a hundred bridges to his name. An amazing person. A fantastic engineering mind. I've had the honor of meeting him a number of times."

The sight of buildings and bridges and physical objects from around the world seemed to energize Patterson. He forgot to introduce me, but I guess Randolph knew I was coming and didn't seem to care.

"And what's this?" Patterson asked, his gaze falling on a model resting on a small table at the center of the room. "I don't recognize it." It seemed to be a campus of buildings, designed in an intriguing combination of a contemporary western Gehry-influenced style and traditional Chinese architecture.

"That's a concept for the China project, the Shenzhen campus," Randolph said.

"What? I've never seen this! Who developed it?"

"I did. With an architect colleague."

"It's fantastic," Patterson said. "Talk me through it."

For the next twenty minutes or so, I listened while Randolph and Patterson moved around, poked at the model and patted it, yammering about volumes and spaces, structures and spans, architectural references and engineering challenges, financing and construction techniques.

When they had exhausted the topic, at least for the moment, Patterson seemed to remember the real reason he had asked to meet with Randolph. He didn't mention the resignation of the provost or the possibility of Alicia filling in. He didn't talk about the vote of no-confidence. Or brag about his latest travels. (The farthest he had gone was to Cleveland, to visit his mother, and he drove.)

He made a simple statement. "Dr. Randolph. At the council meeting you asked me a question. Do you remember what it was?"

"Yes, of course. I asked you about the defining characteristic of this school. Its distinction."

"Yes, and I answered, a little glibly perhaps, something about the fiscal mess we're in."

"Yes, you did."

"Which is true, and I don't retract that. But you went on. You put the question in a different way. You asked me if I understood the school's essential nature. Its true soul."

"Yes, I remember that."

Patterson took a deep breath. I had no idea what to expect from him. Was he going to say that the place was a provincial outpost, a haven of small-minded thinkers, a backwater of outdated educational activity? I didn't think so. Obviously he had done some soul-searching. And he had connected, at least superficially, with Randolph over the Shenzhen vision.

"Well, here's my answer: no. I don't have a sense of Moncrieff's essential nature. And I haven't a clue about its true soul." He paused. Randolph, to his credit, waited, giving Patterson time—whether to hang himself or make a breakthrough, I couldn't be sure.

"But," said Patterson. "I have come to realize that it is my job to understand it. To try to at least."

I could not contain a slight, happy intake of breath.

"That doesn't mean we can keep on doing everything just as we have always done it," Patterson was quick to add. "We both know that won't be possible. Nor does it mean that we shouldn't seek partners for the China project. Or that we don't need a long-range plan."

He paused again. "It does mean that I'm ready for somebody around here to help me out. Teach me what I need to know. Grant me entry to the mysterious and fascinating world of Moncrieff-dom. I am starting to believe that I can't lead us very far without people who know this place better than I do helping to show me the way."

Dr. Randolph raised his eyebrows as if to say, *It's worth a try.* He gestured us into the chairs set around the table with the model campus in the middle.

"Let's sit down," he said. "Have a sherry. And see what we can work out."

EARLY THE NEXT MORNING, I called Owen and filled him in on the meeting with Patterson and Randolph.

"It felt like some real positive movement on Patterson's behalf," I said. "A willingness to listen and engage."

"What about Randolph?"

"He was open to working with Patterson. Overall, I found the meeting encouraging. Oh, and Patterson made the best possible move. He confessed that he does not understand Moncrieff's soul but is willing to learn about it. And what's more, he asked for Randolph's guidance on his journey to enlightenment."

"Well, that is something," Owen replied. "And excellent timing. I've called a meeting of the board's executive committee for next Tuesday, just before the faculty meeting, when the no-confidence resolution might be brought to a vote. The trustees are buzzing. Some are turning against Patterson. They wonder if his presidency is salvageable."

"Why don't you check in with Patterson. Get your take on where he is. Maybe he can attend your meeting to address the board's concerns."

"I'll send him a text right now."

THE FOLLOWING TUESDAY, Patterson did indeed meet with the executive committee, and what had been billed as a "brief check-in" turned into a two-hour, often heated and candid discussion. Committee members expressed their grave concerns about the upcoming faculty meeting. They were worried about the damage that a no-confidence vote could do to his nascent presidency and to Moncrieff. So, they wanted to know, what was Patterson doing to prepare for the meeting? Did he have confidence that he would survive the no-confidence vote? *What was his plan?*

Clearly Patterson did not have a plan. He just couldn't imagine the faculty would vote against him. And what if it did? Other university presidents had been dinged by the faculty and survived, even thrived. A no-confidence vote actually could be clarifying and unifying, he believed. Besides, it had no binding authority. The board was under no obligation to act on a no-confidence vote by the faculty.

"Listen," Patterson said. "I have had some very fruitful conversations with key members of the faculty, including Alicia Chang and Dr. Randolph, and I believe they will speak for me. What's most important," he continued, "is that I have the board's support. *Your support.*"

After further discussion, the executive committee agreed to speak with one voice in support of Ken and touch base with the members of the full board before the meeting.

"However, if the faculty vote goes against you, it will be tougher to keep the board aligned," Roth concluded. "So I suggest you do whatever you can to ensure a positive outcome."

———

THE NEXT EVENING, I slid into a seat at the back of Hamilton Hall, the august space where large campus gatherings were held. Roth, Patterson, and I had agreed that Patterson would not attend the meeting. He was cooling his heels in his office, waiting to hear the result. I listened carefully as faculty members, some three hundred of them, jostled into the hall. The tone of their conversation was largely hostile. I felt a sense of doom in the solemn way the president of the faculty senate, Mehra Patel, called the meeting to order.

"As you know, the purpose of this meeting was to bring to a vote a resolution of no confidence in President Patterson."

Throaty rumbling throughout the room.

"However," Patel continued, "since the initial call for this vote, there have been some further developments. To tell us about them, I want to invite Frank Randolph and Alicia Chang to the stage."

As Randolph and Chang approached the podium, one of the younger faculty members, a comparative literature scholar who had recently arrived on campus, called out.

"I move we call the vote now!"

Patel shook his head. "Just a bit of discussion first."

The scholar stood up. "I move we call the vote now! Is there a second?"

Patel looked uncertain. Randolph and Chang had reached the lectern. Chang leaned into the mic. "I don't believe we've invoked Robert's Rules as of yet." She looked at the young scholar. "With your permission, I'd like to suggest we call a vote on whether to allow discussion."

The young man could not really argue against discussion and agreed. Patel called the vote. It passed. Despite furrowed brows and crossed arms, the faculty seemed willing to listen.

For the next twenty minutes, Randolph and Chang made their case. Yes, Patterson had moved unilaterally and too fast. Yes, he had been uncommunicative and even secretive. Yes, he overstepped by naming himself interim provost. No, this was not the leadership that Moncrieff needed.

"However," Randolph said, "both of us have had discussions with Dr. Patterson and feel that he understands the situation and is now willing to work with us more closely."

"He has agreed to form a task force of faculty and staff to direct the strategic planning process," Alicia added. "And he is open to creating a new position of leadership for the China venture that would most likely come from the engineering school."

Alicia ignored snickering among a group from the language departments, and continued.

"He has also agreed to form two search committees—one to decide, in the very near term, on the appointment of a legitimate interim provost, and a second, larger committee to begin the full-time search for Renee's permanent replacement."

After Randolph and Chang completed their remarks, they opened the floor to questions and comments. There were both. "What is the timetable for the China project? When will the leader be announced? What will the level of faculty involvement be? Is Patterson really the right guy for Moncrieff? Was the board supportive of the president?"

It all came to a head when the young lit scholar waved his hand and stood to pose his question. "Has Patterson figured out whether Moncrieff has a soul and how it might be described?"

The tension melted into laughter.

Randolph spoke softly into the mic. "I'm glad you asked that question. In my conversations with Ken"—Randolph very deliberately chose to use his first name—"he admitted that he could not exactly define the soul of this place."

A few self-righteous snorts could be heard in the audience. Randolph held up his hand.

"But the president said he believed he *should* try to understand it and would try, with our help."

Randolph paused for a moment and looked from face to face. "And I suggest to you that it is a very tough question to answer. Can any one of us say exactly what the defining characteristic of Moncrieff is? Or should be?"

That was the pivotal moment of the evening. There were more comments, questions, concerns, dialogues. At last Phillip Gregory, chair of the philosophy department, stood. He was another of Moncrieff's long-serving faculty members and well respected by all. The room fell silent.

"I think the jury may still be out on our new president," Gregory said calmly, and with a bit of a twinkle in his eye. "I do not know exactly where he wants to lead this institution, or how."

Was he going to call the vote or recommend against it? I couldn't tell.

"However, I propose that we give Dr. Patterson some time to make good on these promises, without having to operate under the cloud of a no-confidence vote. Even if we call a vote and he survives, just the fact of the vote will hang over his head and over the institution as well. Therefore, I urge this eminent group to keep a watchful eye over our enthusiastic president but refrain from calling a vote."

Patel wasted no time in polling the audience and, by a substantial majority, the faculty agreed not to call the question.

———

THE FOLLOWING WEEKS were highly productive. Together, we developed a strategic planning process that would involve the faculty while avoiding the complications the trustees feared. Alicia Chang was named interim provost. Randolph and Patterson met regularly about the China project, refining the physical design and discussing the program offerings. The board put out a statement praising the work of Moncrieff leadership, faculty, and staff in developing the China project, announcing the partnership with the software company, and, most important, officially making Randolph head of the Moncrieff Shenzhen Center for Innovation. Randolph proved to be a very capable academic leader, able to use his standing and influence to accomplish what he needed for himself and for others.

———

ABOUT TWO MONTHS AFTER the fateful faculty meeting, Patterson asked me to join a strategic planning session. "I think you'll find this one quite interesting," he said. I did not ask why. I had learned that his meetings were always quite interesting.

At the meeting, a newly formed faculty group—with members from the business school, the art department, and the political science department—made a presentation. Members had developed a number of innovative and even provocative ways to integrate across their fields to create a new interdisciplinary program that would bring together business, design, and public service.

Patterson listened intently, even gleefully, as they laid out their ideas. Subjects for the curriculum. Research activities. Public events. Collaborations with Chinese businesses, artists, and public figures. Visiting scholars and designers. Marketing and promotion plans. Patterson nodded, chirped, scribbled notes, blurted out the occasional idea or suggestion. But mostly he listened. The faculty seemed genuinely impressed by his openness, his ability to synthesize their ideas and push them further, and his boldness in wanting to take some risks with this program.

After discussion died down for a moment, Patterson stopped the group in its tracks.

"You all recall, I am sure, when Frank asked me that loaded question about whether I believed that Moncrieff had an essential soul, or something like that."

The group smiled and nodded. There were a few smirks.

"Well, I have a loaded question for you. How many of you think the financial troubles we have experienced over the last few years are a momentary blip, and that Moncrieff will return to financial comfort and continue on as it has for our long history?"

Most hands shot up.

"And how many of you think this turbulence is the sign of greater changes to come to higher education, changes that will impact Moncrieff, even with all our assets and resources, and that business as usual for universities will never be quite the same?"

One hand went up, hesitantly.

"This is our main strategic challenge," Patterson stated. "What do we have to do differently to maintain all that is good about this place, and about higher education more broadly? But I know with great conviction that it won't be business as usual."

The group was paying careful attention now, taking in Patterson's point and thinking hard.

As I watched, I had a clear sense that Patterson had caught a glimpse of Moncrieff University's soul, and he was eager to see more.

CHAPTER 7

Leading Leaders

W E HAVE DESCRIBED, through the stories of University Hospital, Quire, and Moncrieff University, how to find the future in the present, how to use influence networks to spread new behaviors, and how to find and strengthen the supports needed to sustain new practices in a world in continuous flux. Now we will turn to what it means to lead in this new world. Leaders are still responsible for creating a vision of what the future will look like and for crafting a viable strategy for realizing that vision—and for adapting as external forces shift.

What is different today?

The social contract between leaders and the workforce is changing as the economic context has changed. People over the course of their working lives will hold multiple jobs with multiple organizations—even pursue multiple careers. Consequently their primary loyalty will go to their personal development and career, ahead of loyalty to any one company and its leaders. They are also used to working with greater autonomy and freedom than ever before—and contemporary approaches to management encourage this autonomy.

These developments are turning employees into what are essentially temporary workers, who collectively resemble a volunteer workforce, almost a volunteer army. The challenge for leaders is to keep the workforce interested and committed while putting strategy into action. To do that, leaders need to align and mobilize people so that their individual talents and efforts clearly contribute to the organization's overall performance.

It's no longer enough for a leader to get the strategy right (a daunting task in itself) and then expect her lieutenants to execute it. The cultural rules for interaction inside organizations, specifically the ways people are obliged to work with each other that we discussed in Chapter 5, don't embrace that kind of leadership anymore. In the new organizational environment—with its need for speed, innovation, growth, and ever-improving productivity, a volunteer army whose members are self-motivated can be an enormous asset.

This does not look much like the world in which many of us learned how to lead. In this chapter, we'll look at three cultural shifts that affect how leaders operate today.

The first shift is in organizational structure. In tightly coupled organizations people at the top make decisions about strategy and resource allocation, and then they delegate follow-through to others in the middle and the front lines. Tightly coupled hierarchies are shifting toward more loosely coupled ways of working, which require different cultural agreements and rules for interaction. In loosely coupled organizations, individual units have more autonomy in how they make decisions and execute strategy.[1]

The second shift is from autonomy and control to interdependence and collaboration, from "push" strategies and techniques for getting work done, to "pull" strategies and techniques. This shift has economic ramifications and is occurring both locally and globally. A cultural shift is taking place within and between organizations, and it is more difficult for individuals or business units within companies to create value by themselves.

The third shift relates to motivation. A leader once was supposed to motivate and "empower" followers. While the intentions were good, the approach did not work so well. A good deal of research shows that people cannot really motivate others; we motivate ourselves. We are, in effect, our own leaders, which is why we talk about "leading leaders." Your task as a leader is to identify the things that motivate people—their interests and passions—and connect them to the change you're trying to create.

From Tightly to Loosely Coupled

Tightly coupled and loosely coupled organizations have different sets of agreements for getting work done, rules for how people work together, and implications for leaders. Whether an organization is tightly or loosely coupled is determined by certain characteristics: the way different parts of an organization are connected to the whole; the way leadership and authority are distributed; and the ways in which decisions are made.

In tightly coupled organizations, people are appointed to positions of authority, usually by those above them in a hierarchy. Vertical alignment from the top down connects all of the organizational elements—departments, functions, business units—in the service of a set of objectives shared by all. This doesn't mean that all is peace and harmony internally—tightly coupled organizations are often designed to foster internal competition—but resources are aligned toward achieving the defined objectives. In the Army, for example, the objective is called a mission. Distribution of authority and responsibility—the chain of command—is clear and executed through hierarchical relationships from the top down in order to achieve the mission. Tightly coupled organizations have been ubiquitous for so long that they seem "normal."

Loosely coupled organizations operate differently. In universities, academic medical centers, associations, and court systems, for example, different parts of an organization often have different objectives and, at times, different missions. An academic medical center has multiple missions and multiple divisions, differentially devoted to research, teaching, clinical care, and community engagement. The objectives of one may stand in opposition to the others. Researchers live in a different occupational culture than most clinicians, for example. Research focuses on discovering new knowledge. Clinicians focus on diagnosing and treating patients. Research takes much longer from start to completion of a project than fast-paced clinical work. Clinical departments, for example, sometimes find themselves competing for resources devoted to bench research that they believe would be better devoted to direct patient care.

In state courts, another loosely coupled system, judicial supreme court leaders may have objectives that are very different from those of administrative court leaders. And both may have objectives that differ from the state bar association. Yet all three come together to comprise the judiciary function as the third branch of government in the United States.

IN LOOSELY COUPLED ORGANIZATIONS, leaders hold titles to positions, which make those organizations appear to be tightly coupled. In loosely coupled organizations, however, the authority that comes with a position is often limited. Most leaders in loosely coupled systems must earn authority through building trust and collaborating with others. An administrative leader of a trial court, for example, may have an important title that puts him on a par with most court justices. But he is often not a judge or even a lawyer, that is, not a member of those two identity groups. Consequently, the administrator likely holds little sway over a judge who believes he works only for the chief justice, even when the organizational chart shows he reports to the administrator as well.

While a senior-level position indicates a level of leadership, it is a necessary but not sufficient authorization to lead. Leaders who do not have strong negotiation, collaboration, and influence skills may not survive long in loosely coupled systems. To be effective, they have to work with others to find shared interests

in order to move forward together, or, as is often the case, negotiate their way through multiple competing interests. We saw
the challenges Kenneth Patterson faced at Moncrieff University.
Patterson thought that recognizing what needed to be done and
then putting together a plan for accomplishing it was enough,
and that others would come along. But in a university setting,
faculty leadership has a lot of power, and faculty members have
a lot of autonomy. Telling faculty members what to do rarely
succeeds, and leaders need to use other ways to influence change
and move things forward. Patterson had not earned the respect
and authority that came with his position, especially among faculty whose support he would need to be successful. The cultural
rules for interacting with faculty were not detailed in the employee handbook or displayed on a wall plaque. They were tacit
cultural agreements about the exchange of ideas, about reciprocity, and about obligations that those in leadership positions have
to other members of the organizational community.

In organizations of all shapes and sizes, people collaborate
through social networks as much as they do through formal
organizational structures, and need to do so in order to get their
work done. As we saw at Quire, the power to propel or stifle
change often lies in a leader's ability to tap into informal communication networks and work effectively with strong influencers, like Norbert Ball.

At Moncrieff University, Kenneth Patterson discovered
he couldn't simply come up with a good idea and expect others to follow him. He had to find ways to match his ideas to
the interests of others in order to be successful. Using formal

organizational channels alone was not enough. He had to learn how social networks inside the university worked, and identify allies who were strong influencers. That led him to Alicia Chang and then Frank Randolph, whom other faculty respected and consulted about the upcoming no-confidence vote.

Your reaction may be, "I've been living this movie for years," or "This doesn't apply to our organization," but a closer understanding of how this works from a cultural perspective and its implications for leaders can be useful.

IMPLICATIONS FOR LEADERS

What consequences do leaders experience as organizations shift from being tightly to more loosely coupled and networked? How can paying attention to those implications lead to improved performance? There are three patterns that occur as part of the shift from tighter to looser coupling:

- Organizational boundaries become more permeable and have to be managed differently.
- The exercise of authority that comes with successful leadership works differently in loosely coupled systems: you have to give authority to others in order to get it back.
- While some final decisions remain in the wheelhouse of those in leadership positions, decision making becomes a distributed team endeavor in loosely coupled systems.

BOUNDARIES INSIDE ORGANIZATIONS, between functions, departments, and business units, and the boundaries between an organization and its wider environment of suppliers, competitors, and customers, are becoming more permeable—transactions and relationships between these units are more fluid and customary. Cross-boundary collaboration is becoming the norm rather than the exception when creating solutions to business problems, and this has consequences for leaders.

We believe the increasingly permeable nature of organizational boundaries is at least partially a response to the turbulence and disruptive change we face in the economic and social environment. With an increase in turbulence comes an increased demand for companies to collaborate more effectively and quickly across silos inside their organization, and with outside partners and allies as well.[2] Organizations of all types increasingly work in multifunctional teams and with outside partners to develop ways to meet changing customer demands. Working across boundaries helps solve challenging problems and at the same time brings with it increased complexity.

At one end of the value chain, companies are asking more of their suppliers, and at the other end are including their customers in the design and delivery of products and services. IKEA began to ride this wave early on. The company encourages customers to participate in the design, delivery, and installation of products, and they have done a great job outsourcing the latter two functions to all of us who drive home and assemble their furniture. Similarly, financial institutions offer personalized banking, and along the way shift the burden of managing accounts from the bank to customers through online supports. Endless numbers of apps enable us to take on work once done by "middlemen,"often cutting out or reinventing the role of entire businesses. (Think travel agents and bank tellers.)

These new arrangements allow companies to increase their flexibility and rearrange their distribution of labor. Value is created less in a chain from one link to the next, from supplier through designer and maker to user, and more in a constellation of players, more of an ecosystem of relationships in which any one participant can affect another and help other members of the ecosystem create value. This allows participants to pull resources across the boundaries of their organization and create value in collaboration with others.[3]

To stay competitive in this collaborative environment, loosely coupled systems pull together the talent, ideas, and resources needed to solve a problem as the problem appears. At Quire, sales and business development people brought software design engineers to their customer sales calls, inviting customers to become part of the software design process. As boundaries become more permeable, people in many parts of an organization find opportunities to take on leadership roles—whatever their position in the formal hierarchy may be. The more you help them develop their leadership abilities, the more adept your organization can become at making cultural shifts during turbulent times. Success in doing this depends a great deal on your ability to lend your authority to others to get work done.

IT GOES WITHOUT SAYING that a leader exercises authority to get work done. However, as organizations become loosely coupled, the way authority works is being redefined. Important questions arise: What does it mean to lead? Who gets to lead? Where does authority come from? The definition of authority and its execution are in flux.

It's not surprising that questions about authority and how it operates are emerging as many organizations shift from tight to loose coupling. Things seemed a lot clearer when authority came from appointed positions. When University Hospital made its shift from the surgeon as captain of the ship to a team-based approach that encouraged all members of the team to use their authority to speak up whenever there was a problem, great confusion resulted. When Ken Patterson announced his plans for a campus in China, he was acting on the basis of a set of cultural agreements that were applicable to a tightly coupled organization, like the one he had led previously. Once again, one set of cultural agreements clashed with another.

Leaders in both organizations learned that authority to lead comes as much from others as it comes from one's formal position. Patterson increased his authority by including the board and faculty leadership in his deliberations. At University Hospital, Dr. Green strengthened his authority by distributing it, inviting others on the OR team to identify and solve problems and make recommendations about how to improve patient outcomes. He distributed his authority to others in order to get it back from them.

Leaders in a fast-changing world need followers who are

passionate rather than compliant. One of the best ways to attract people with passion is to create opportunities for them to take up leadership and exercise their own authority. Ironically, the more you do this, the more your own authority expands. On the way to becoming a leader, the primary task is to learn how to get work done with and through others. As a leader, your primary task shifts from developing yourself to developing others, from leading followers to leading leaders. As one of our colleagues likes to say, "It's time to stop being a hero and start creating heroes."

By sharing authority with others, you can tap into the energy and passion they bring to work, both of which expand as they see how their part connects to the whole of what you are working to accomplish, the picture on the jigsaw puzzle box. When others hear that you are on the lookout for opportunities for people to take up leadership, news spreads that you are a leader worth following. You become a "multiplier."[4] Opportunities to authorize others show up nowhere more powerfully than in how decisions are made.

WHEN LEADERS BEGIN to share their authority with others, agreements about how decisions are made come to the fore. When you, as the leader, invite another person to take on more authority, how far does that authority go? What kinds of decisions are included in the person's new responsibility? To be effective, leaders need to make decisions in ways that promote the exercise of authority by others in a disciplined and flexible manner while keeping the voluntary army engaged. By helping nascent leaders make good decisions, you can help them improve their leadership skills and also leverage your own authority; the quality of leadership in the organization increases.

When we use the term "decision making," we are not referring only to the person who says yes or no to finalize a decision. Rather, we define decision making as the work required to make the best possible decision. Whether that decision is small or large, it often requires collaboration across functions, departments, and other silos. Speed and agility in decision making demand fluid, skillful collaboration and negotiation across those boundaries. This means knowing enough about what other parts of the organization do, especially those where collaboration can remove obstacles and improve productivity.

KING CHEMICAL, a $500 million family business based in Albany, New York, faced a challenge that required a shift from an autonomous and controlling style of leadership to one based on interdependence and collaboration. Over a period of ten years, King Chemical had tripled its revenues, and its CEO, Jason Bradley, attributed the company's success to one factor: his personal, passionate attention to decision making. Bradley involved himself in virtually every management decision, from major matters of strategy to minor details such as the purchase of office supplies.

King Chemical was founded in the early 1950s by Isaac King, Bradley's grandfather, to manufacture and wholesale one of the earliest of the nontoxic cleaning compounds. The timing was right: home sales were booming and a clean house was of great social importance. Businesses, too, were sprouting up everywhere and they all needed office cleaning supplies. Isaac King was able to purchase, at a very good price, a manufacturing facility that had produced wartime goods, and his business was on its way.

King Chemical did not lack for competitors. Isaac King knew he needed a competitive advantage beyond his products and decided that it would come from his scrupulous attention to management detail. One of his practices was to make regular personal visits to his customers and sometimes he would take his grandson Jason along with him. Jason Bradley remembers that Grandfather King would rattle off endless details about his customers: every product they bought, what they used it for, how much they spent, how much profit King Chemical made. At first, it was far too much information for young Jason to absorb. Eventually, however, he began to see that his grandfather's management approach worked extremely well. With each visit, Isaac King would make an important connection with customers. He would listen to their feedback about how the King products were working. He asked questions about their business, how they were faring, what they needed. Jason could see that his grandfather really cared about his products and his customers and that the customers had a lot of loyalty to their supplier. After each visit, the elder King would talk about what he had learned and how it would help him make important decisions about the business.

It was during those rides with his grandfather that Jason Bradley got hooked on the family business. He started working for the company when he was still in high school, starting out in the warehouse and steadily working his way up. He went at the business in exactly the same way his grandfather did. He kept tabs on every purchase, tracked every order, knew every customer by name, made sure King's prices were competitive, and responded to every service issue. Over the years, King Chemical grew slowly and surely, and Jason Bradley eventually moved into the CEO position. Grandfather Isaac retired, proud of what his company and his grandson had accomplished.

In the early 2000s, Bradley saw an opportunity to move beyond wholesaling and expand into retail. It was a big move and he knew he couldn't pull it off with the managers who were running the wholesale operation. He went about building a new management team the way he did everything else: carefully, methodically, and with close personal attention to every detail. King Chemical had an excellent reputation and Bradley was persuasive about the opportunity that awaited.

Bradley assembled an impressive group of six seasoned managers, some of whom came from King's main competitors and some from different industries. Most of them had worked in companies larger than King, multibillion dollar operations, and had impressive titles, lots of formal authority, and managed large staffs. The ones who joined King were attracted by Bradley's hands-on approach and the fast-paced entrepreneurial environment. They left their slow-moving, bureaucratic companies because they wanted to be directly engaged in making decisions that contributed to the growth of the company.

Almost as soon as the new team arrived, things started going wrong. First off, they couldn't engage as a team. Decision making was a disaster. Either decisions were made without enough deliberation or they took forever and turned out badly. Two managers left within six months of arriving. Bradley pushed a third one out the door. The transition from wholesale to retail stalled.

The CFO, Kevin Mancuso, who had been with King for many years, watched as things unraveled. He had seen managers come and go and didn't worry when a management team didn't work perfectly together, but this was different. This was full-out management dysfunction and it was hurting the business. King Chemical was losing sales and customers.

Bradley trusted Mancuso and asked him for help. What was going on? Mancuso suggested that an outside perspective could be useful and that's when we got involved. We spent time at the company, listening in and shadowing several members of the senior management team. The problem quickly became clear. Jason Bradley was conducting business just as he always had, just as his grandfather always had. He still got involved in every decision and kept track of every detail. He decided how many products to launch in the new retail business each year. He reviewed the pricing of every contract. He got involved in determining the most efficient way to load trucks. He decided when shipments should be made. He responded personally to service problems. He made autonomous decisions that sometimes caused problems for other executives. For example, King lost an important customer relationship because a product shipment was late. Why? Bradley had rerouted the truck to make a small delivery to a longtime customer. With so much of their attention focused on operational details, the new management team was unable to focus on the big issues. One day when we asked for a pad of paper, we discovered that Bradley kept the only key to the office supply closet.

Everybody on the team was frustrated, including Bradley. "These guys don't understand the consequences of their decisions," he told us. "They seem to think they're still working in a big bureaucracy. Nobody talks to anybody else. My sales executive doesn't check in with the head of manufacturing to make sure he can actually deliver on orders. The manufacturing guy doesn't check in with our logistics exec. They perform their own jobs fine, I guess, but they don't make any connections between their role and the roles of others. And I get caught in the middle when things go wrong. I'm the guy who has to decide everything. I'm the guy who has to talk the customer off the ledge."

King Chemical was stuck, unable to move from the way it had done business for fifty years—very successfully—to a new approach. We knew Jason Bradley would have to see that his senior team members could take on the authority he wanted to give them. It would be easy to say that Bradley didn't know how to delegate and wasn't willing to give up control, but the problem went deeper than that. King Chemical had a strong culture and history of success, and that was now threatened. Jason saw no reason to change his behavior if his new managers couldn't connect their parts of the business to the whole. From his point of view, once he saw that his people took the role of company stewardship seriously, he would consider changing his behavior.

We thought that Bradley's decision-making style was also a factor affecting the business in a negative way. To explore how this worked, we asked Mancuso, the CFO, to help us identify an important problem that would affect most of the senior executives and that might be confounded by Bradley's traditional approach to decision making. Mancuso told us that he had just gotten off the phone with one of King's biggest customers, who had informed him it was going to shop around for a new supplier. The shipments from King were always late and the company couldn't properly service its own customers as a result. King had two weeks to get things right or that was it. This was a real and urgent problem and one that affected almost all members of the senior management team.

We met with the senior managers, intending to propose this approach to them, but first opened the floor to general discussion. We listened carefully as they told us what was wrong with Bradley, and then we gave them feedback about what we had heard from Bradley about them. There was some defensiveness and venting and we let it go on for a few minutes. Then we suggested that, as a way to improve the decision-making process, we take up a real problem and work through it in a collaborative way.

But what problem should it be? Kevin Mancuso told them about the big client that was getting ready to bolt. Suddenly we had everybody's full attention. Determining the root cause of the problem didn't take long. It had to do with the transfer of materials and products among three of King's plants. Who made the decisions about these transfers? We got blank stares. Finally one of the managers spoke up. "Each plant has its own process for making transfers. The plant foremen report to me, but there's no unified system across the facilities." So then we asked, "What do you do when there's a transfer problem?" Another managed chuckled. "I do what we all do. I go to Bradley. He helps troubleshoot the problem. We get back to work." The other managers agreed that's how they all worked. They thought Bradley wanted it that way.

Next we asked how the process could be improved. The answer was obvious: develop a single transfer procedure for all the company facilities. Why hadn't this been done? It was Bradley's fault, of course. But had they ever proposed an alternative? No. Did they think they could come up with something better? Hell yes. Would Bradley stand in the way of putting a better process in place? That remained to be seen.

Over the next several weeks, we worked with the management team (minus Bradley) to figure out what decisions went into creating a transfer system that would work for the whole company. First, each senior manager learned more about what the others did and then shared the knowledge with their direct reports. As they developed the new transfer system, they realized that lines of authority would have to shift during the process. There would not be a sole decision maker or owner of the entire process. One of them would take the lead at some times and, at other points along the way, would follow the lead of colleagues.

This development process brought the senior managers closer together. After six weeks, they were making decisions much more effectively than they ever had, and were ready to present their approach to Bradley. Amazingly enough, it was the first time the senior managers had asked to meet with their CEO as a group.

Bradley, uncharacteristically, was nervous. What were they up to? Was this going to be a rebellion? Were they all going to quit? Maybe the consultants had cooked something up? Kevin Mancuso assured him that the managers were working on a business problem and wanted to present a solution to him. Still, Bradley was uncertain. He had always met with his executives one on one and didn't know what to expect.

After a bit of uncomfortable banter, the managers stepped up and made their proposal. The new process required them to work collaboratively across silos—the company's divisions that had a tendency to act like isolated units. All of the managers would participate in key decisions, and they had worked out who would have authority at every step along the way. Bradley was not only impressed but delighted. Team members were working together, talking to one another, showing their stewardship of the entire company, not just their department. To his credit, he told them on the spot how pleased he was, and authorized them to put the plan into action. His final comment floored everybody. "Let's meet as a group more often. That hasn't been my way, I know. So I might get a little uncomfortable at times. But you guys have come up with something good here. We need more of that. What do you say?"

Not surprisingly, the senior management team of King Chemical said yes, and within eighteen months the company was starting to make inroads into the targeted retail market. No customers were threatening to leave over botched shipments. New customers were coming on board. And Jason Bradley had taken the lock off the office supply cabinet and thrown away the key.

When you're leading leaders, they have to be able to make decisions that don't all bounce back to you. At the same time, it doesn't make sense to relinquish control and delegate authority to others unless they can see the ways that most leadership decisions engage and affect other people and units beyond their part of the organization. This means leaders of a volunteer army face a double task: to help others learn what they need to know to understand the consequences of a decision and then take smart risks to share authority with them. Accomplishing these tasks is often a lot more challenging than it may seem at first. You're taking a risk when you relinquish control, especially of the things you care most about—as are others when they take up their authority knowing that failure may ensue if their recommendations are incorrect.

What is the value in making this shift?

- Increased speed and agility in making the best decisions possible (especially across increasingly permeable boundaries).

- Using all the expertise available to you as a leader; others learn to lead, which frees up your time to focus on strategically important issues.
- Others experience the challenges, risks, and responsibilities of leadership in realistic ways; they build loyalty to you because they're volunteers in this new world who are responsible for managing their own careers.

When leading leaders, distributing authority makes sense. Then others become resources that can help you pull new practices through the organization. You won't need to push when others are pulling.

Moving from Push to Pull

The idea that we are making a transition from push to pull is not new. The economics of the transition have been well documented by researchers like John Seely Brown and John Hagel[5] as well as social psychologists like Barry Schwartz.[6] The transition is a cultural one that shows up inside organizations as well as between them, for example, in the way parts of an organization try on new ways of working to solve customer problems. At King Chemical, Jason Bradley had to pull sales, programming, shipping, receiving, and billing together in a way that helped each understand the other's roles and how each part connected to the whole operation. Boundaries between their departments had to become more permeable in order to meet customer expectations and to enable the company to grow. Engineers at Quire pulled together found pilots from different parts of the company to create a networked approach to knowledge management. Creating pull helps connect the parts of a company to the whole to meet customer demands.

We see signs of the shift from push to pull every day as leaders in all sorts of companies realize they can be more successful more quickly using that approach. At Quire, Gus learned how best to adapt Six Sigma and make it an attractive set of tools for increasing profitable revenue by listening to his internal customers. One of the nurses at University Hospital discovered she could free up time to concentrate on patients by giving them her cell phone number. They were less anxious when they knew they could call and get her attention right away. As a result they called less often, allowing her to concentrate on whichever patient she was with at the time.

Building a coalition, as Gus did at Quire, creates pull by mobilizing people's energy and passion to turn individual found pilots into strong practices. The third generation of the Volz family was able to pull the second and third generations of the family together by forming a coalition, the Family Unity Committee. When Kenneth Patterson realized that the dean's council could become a potential coalition of allies, he began to see how it could help him achieve the China project. Initially he saw the council as an obstacle to work around, hoping that it would eventually see the wisdom of his ideas. He rediscovered his authority by using the constraints he faced as opportunities instead of shackles.

ONE OF THE MOST EFFECTIVE WAYS to create pull for a new behavior is to influence the behavior of someone who can influence the person you are actually targeting. Mothers Against Drunk Driving (MADD), for example, has used this approach very successfully. In its Friends Don't Let Friends Drive Drunk campaign, MADD "aims around the target" by asking friends of the main target of the campaign to make sure that they don't let people they care about drive under the influence of alcohol.

This technique, often called "triangulating," can help you reach those you want to influence but who are in groups that disagree with what you're trying to accomplish. Skeptical friends play a particularly important boundary-spanning role here. Recall the Family Unity Committee that served as a coalition for the Volz family. The committee found that skeptical friends like Emily acted as an early warning system by raising objections and questions that those opposed to a governance structure would raise. The committee could test ideas in advance with Emily, and she could then identify those the committee would need to influence to move forward. And in many cases Emily could help influence them herself.

RESEARCH ON HOW TO CHANGE ingrained habits shows that people who agree to a small commitment are much more likely to make a larger one later on.[7] So, set your bar for participation low and then make it easy for people to scale up. If you ask people to commit to just one or two specific goals over a clearly defined period of time, it's easier to set new and more ambitious goals after the first small goals have been attained.

A sales manager at Rockledge Insurance, Bill Starfield, used this technique masterfully in changing the behavior of his sales agents. He would begin by tapping into a salesperson's passion, asking him what he most enjoyed doing. Playing golf was a common answer. Bill wouldn't even raise the terms "accountability" or "results" at work. Instead, he would suggest that he could help the sales agent spend more time golfing. They would set monthly golf objectives, and Bill would help his salesperson meet them. When the salesperson went off track, he'd be there to help him get back on track by asking him to make small commitments that made more time for golf.

After a few months, Bill would pivot from focusing on golf and ask what brought the person into sales, what he hoped to achieve, and would build from there. Bill and the agent would set weekly and monthly results-based sales targets, and followed the same steps he had when working with the agent to improve his golf game. Again he would start with small commitments and build on them. Many, many successful sales agents counted Bill Starfield as their mentor, and in turn used his technique of starting with incremental commitments to train others. Bill didn't talk about the importance of accountability or hover over people to make sure they were doing what they were supposed to do. He created pull for them to hold themselves accountable.

MOTIVATION STILL MATTERS BUT LOOKS DIFFERENT

To be successful, leaders need followers. But the culture of organizational life has changed, and with it the relationship between leaders and followers. Leaders now expect managers and employees to function on a variety of project teams with a great deal of authority, autonomy, and self-direction, often without the kind of hierarchical supports that once existed.[8] And most people want this level of autonomy and self-direction to feel that they are able to put their good ideas to work and are appreciated for doing so. Organizations are leaner and spans of control often broader. Matrix structures lend additional complexity and work best when people negotiate decisions effectively with their peers at lower levels in the organization and avoid the added cost and lost time when decisions are delegated back up the chain of command. And in loosely coupled organizations, people have a great deal of autonomy and control over their time and efforts.

Motivation, however, still matters. As organizations become more loosely coupled and networked, people throughout the workforce have more ways to build relationships that help them act as leaders of their own careers. As leaders work to engage followers, motivation works differently. Recent research suggests that motivation is not something that one does "to" another. We don't motivate or persuade each other, as much as we motivate and persuade ourselves. This means that we as leaders can be as convincing as possible, but motivation only occurs when a connection is made between our interests and the interests of those we would like to feel motivated to join us.[9]

Mobilizing a workforce of people who are in effect volunteers working on their own development while employed in your company is not an easy task. Ironically, it's easy to work too hard at it. If you find yourself trying to convince people to follow your lead because you believe it's the right thing to do, or because it makes sense based on a strong value proposition, you may be pushing too hard. Building a business case, for example, is necessary to show managers and employees why changing their behavior is critical. But that alone is unlikely to motivate them to change. Davidian and Crowley knew the business case for change at University Hospital, as did Ken Patterson and the board at Moncrieff University. But that understanding took them only as far as the starting line. If you believe that making the case rationally and clearly is enough, the person you're convincing the most may be yourself.

Understanding how motivation works can help you establish strong, influential connections. Study after study, from psychologists such as Abraham Maslow, who introduced a theory of motivation based on a hierarchy of needs,[10] to behavioral economists like Richard Thaler[11] and Dan Ariely,[12] has identified multiple motivations that inform why we work.

Building on these ideas, Daniel Pink suggests that for people who are not paid enough to live on or perform repetitive, mechanical jobs, making enough money is often the primary motivator.[13] This is not unlike Maslow's hierarchy, in which basic physiological needs and safety conditions must be met before there is room to focus on taking steps toward self-esteem and self-actualization. Pink goes on to explain that once people are paid a self-described "good enough" wage in their job and basic conditions of safety have been met, three things motivate them: the opportunity to be self-directed, the chance to master something, and the opportunity to be part of an organization that has a purpose.[14] A leader cannot command someone to be motivated through these levers but can create the conditions where people are likely to "feel motivated" because they are motivating themselves.

CONNECTING YOUR PASSION TO THE PASSION OF OTHERS

Novelist and poet E. M. Forster famously wrote, "Only connect." Leadership is as simple, and as complicated, as that. To create pull for what you want to accomplish, connect your passion to the passions and interests of others. Your own passions and interests are important as well, but when you are leading leaders, connecting to their passions and interests can turn compliance into commitment.

Connecting your passion to the passion of others in ways they find motivating is perhaps the core task of those who find themselves leading in the midst of the shifts we've talked about: from tightly coupled hierarchies to loosely coupled networks, the shift from pushing to pulling new practices through the organization, and the shift from motivating others to connecting with what motivates them.

We can describe this new style of leadership, which includes connecting your passion to the passion of others, as "command and collaborate"—a combination of the traditional "command

and control" and the new drive toward collaborative leadership. This may sound like an oxymoron, but the two ideas are
complementary in the context of leading leaders. To lead an
organization through cultural shifts that result in new practices
that stick, you need to command *and* collaborate.

In a loosely coupled organization, a seeming liability—not
being able to operate in a command-and-control mode—can turn
into an asset, with people throughout the organization making
decisions that connect their part to the whole, and their behavior
and interests to your vision. You have to slow down at first to
make this work, but the investment soon propels the organization
forward with increasing velocity, as Jason discovered at King
Chemical. As his senior managers became a team, they were able
to boost the productivity of the entire company, which in turn
freed him up to spend more time in the market and plan ahead.

We have focused on the collaborative function of leadership—
discovering the future in the present through found pilots,
building a coalition to help create supports for new practices,
building social capital by identifying influencers who can expand your social networks, aligning your interests and passions
with those of others.

Where does the command function come in? Many people
have made the case that old, crusty hierarchical organizations
don't work, that the command-and-control style of leadership
needs to yield to one that emphasizes collaboration only. The
implication is that command cannot exist without control, and
that command is simply about telling people what to do and

then trying to put in controls to make sure they do it. These definitions equate command with a kind of dictatorial disregard for the capabilities of others.

That is not, however, how the authority to command works as organizations become more loosely coupled, pulling needed resources together to create and support new practices. When leading leaders, there is, perhaps ironically, an increased demand for commanding leadership. Leaders command in a different way, though, by creating a commanding presence and a commitment to developing the capabilities of others throughout the organization. As Gus at Quire put it, "I'm not responsible for assuring you that you'll have a job in the future, but I am responsible for helping you develop the skills and competencies you'll need to step into your next job."

To build a commanding presence in organizations that are reshaping themselves, focus on two central tasks: protect the organization by keeping it within its safety zone during times of cultural transition, and guide and direct the organization as a conductor artfully leads an orchestra.

The wake-up call that comes with un-ignorable moments puts these two tasks front and center. To keep the organization in its safety zone in a rapidly changing environment, create early warning systems to identify and prepare for the internally driven resistance and externally driven challenges that accompany cultural transition. Prepare for the inevitability of being stuck and build capabilities to leverage the power of stuckness in order to get unstuck. To guide the organization, manage the tensions and contradictions facing the organization—the tension between old established ways of working and new emerging practices.

Those on the leadership team at University Hospital learned this in no uncertain terms. They knew they could not afford more of those moments that occurred with the missing sponge in the operating room, especially given the relentless regulatory and economic pressures they faced to simultaneously reduce cost and improve the quality of care. At the same time, they knew that talking about the need to command and collaborate was easier than putting the talk into action. The power of old command-and-control habits, supported in all sorts of unspoken ways, turned out to be difficult to break. Crowley and Davidian knew they needed new cultural agreements about how work gets done, and about how people work with each other to get that work done. At first, they did not know how to get out of their own way to make that happen, but they learned quickly.

It took a couple of years for the leadership team at University Hospital to make the transition from command and control to command and collaborate, just as it took time for Ken Patterson, with the help of others, to make that transition at Moncrieff University. In each case, slowing down initially made it possible to propel the organizations forward more quickly over the long run.

Learning to understand the cultural shifts already under way—the shift from tight to loosely coupled systems, how to create pull, and the ways motivation works now—helped them identify and execute those shifts. In both cases, it was impossible to move a new strategy forward without understanding the power and importance of cultural identity, the answer to what Frank Randolph, the chair of the engineering department and leader of the Moncrieff Shenzhen Center for Innovation, called the soul question. "What do you consider to be the single, most distinctive and distinguishing characteristic of your organization? Its essential nature? Its true soul?"

The answer to this question lies in understanding your culture, the strongest driver to a successful future.

Conclusion

What Is Our Future?

I T HAS BEEN TWENTY YEARS since Bee Lor's funeral, and almost thirty since we worked with Bee and other members of the Hmong community in Philadelphia. Over the years we have remained "American friends," attending some important community and family events, staying in touch at a distance.

Much has changed for the Hmong over thirty years, and much has remained the same. What's different? Many have moved out of the city, seeking jobs, opportunities, and new lives in other parts of the country. Those who have stayed have grown older, married, raised families. Some found jobs in the civil sector or community organizations. Others have opened restaurants, become engineers, worked in software companies,

founded their own companies. Many of the younger generation have gone to college and graduate school. What remains
the same? Essential elements of the Hmong culture: a strong
work ethic and belief system, social agreements that include
respect for the authority of elders, community rituals, and more.
In other words, we see a community that has developed new
strategies for success based on traditional ways of doing things.

This is most strikingly evident in the story of Pang Xiong
Sirirathasuk Sikoun. We first met her in the 1980s when she
was just starting to establish herself in America. She, along with
other members of the Hmong community, had fled to Laos after
the Vietnam War, lived in a tent city there for years, then made
their way through France to the United States. When she and
her family arrived, Pang Xiong did not speak English, and had
little sense of the culture—the way things get done around here.

Pang Xiong knew she had to find a new way to make a
living, but her main marketable skill was the discipline of *paj
ntaub*, a traditional Hmong technique of embroidery and fine
sewing. She tried to sell her work but had few takers. Gradually
she adapted the embroidery to better suit American tastes and
had a little success. But it clearly wouldn't be enough to support
her for a lifetime.

Then she stumbled onto a possible solution. She heard about
the Amish quilters in central Pennsylvania and the huge market
they had built for their amazing handiwork. People come from
all over the world to the Amish farmland of Lancaster County,
Pennsylvania, to purchase the quilts, and these practical works
of art hang in museums worldwide. Pang Xiong was intrigued

by the quilters and their quilts. She did a little investigation, used her social skills to connect with the Amish, and eventually was able to collaborate with them. Pang Xiong then adapted her style to make embroidered pieces the Amish could include as sections in their patterned quilts.

It was, in a way, a found pilot for the Amish as well as for Pang Xiong. Pang Xiong had uncovered a new way of working within a larger social organization. Once she grasped what the Amish were doing and adapted her skills to their ways, she was able to apply the learning and build her own business. She found new applications for the *paj ntaub* technique and created a whole range of products: distinctive pillows, bed-spreads, jackets, wall hangings, and baby carriers. Eventually the Amish asked Pang Xiong to do more than just contribute panels to their work—to sew the quilts as well. Over the years, she built a thriving business. Eventually most Amish quilters recognized the skills the Hmong brought to quilting. When you buy an Amish quilt now, there's a good chance that it was sewn by Hmong craftswomen.

Today Pang Xiong lives with her extended family in a large house in Upper Darby, a Philadelphia suburb. It's only a few miles from the neighborhood in West Philadelphia where the Hmong had settled thirty years ago, but the move marked a ma-jor cultural shift in social class for Pang Xiong and her family—from the status of urban refugees who spoke no English and, like many refugee communities, experienced poverty and racism, to gradually learning how to survive in the United States, working their way to middle-class stability—all in one generation.

Pang Xiong's dining room is piled high with inventory, work that she, along with her extended family and other women in the community, have produced for sale in stores, as well as at craft fairs, farmers markets, and folk festivals. Pang Xiong is not only a successful business owner but also a Hmong community leader. Her home is often crowded with young Hmong women who work with her in the business and are being trained in sewing *paj ntaub*. While they work together, they get an earful of her wisdom and a belly full of her wonderful Hmong cooking.

The skills that Pang Xiong has developed are much the same as those needed by leaders in twenty-first century organizations: resilience in the face of continuous change, the ability to influence others and build social capital (through her network of American friends as well as inside the Hmong community), strategically using social networks to expand the reach of the business, and skillfully employing culture as a renewable resource—in her case, adapting Hmong textile designs and colors to American tastes.

Pang Xiong, in her sewing business and as a community leader, has found answers to the four questions we posed in the Introduction:

> *What is our identity as an organization?*
> *Who's in charge?*
> *How do I lead?*
> *What is our future?*

Every leader today must also respond to them.

THE FOURTH QUESTION

You must answer the first three questions before you can answer the fourth one. If you don't know how your culture works, are unsure of who's in charge, can't describe the identity of your organization, and can't command *and* collaborate, you will not have the ability or will to craft new agreements about how work gets done in order propel your organization forward.

But even as you find answers to the first three questions—and as new ways of working emerge and start to take root—the fourth question still hangs in there: *What is our future?*

As industrial age organizations come apart at the seams, should we expect totally new organizational forms to emerge? Will the traditional organization unravel completely and disappear? How will organizations be affected by new technologies, social media, and the disruption of many traditional industries? Will boundaries between and among companies and their suppliers, partners, and other organizations—community groups, government agencies, consultancies—become so permeable as to disappear? What about the workforce? Will the next generation have any interest in working within structured organizations? Already, young people seem to work and adapt in continuous motion, shifting rapidly from one project to another, from one group to another, forming networked communities of the committed and engaged as they go. Already, we see companies operating in similar ways—with teams and task forces forming to solve a business problem or create a new business unit, and then disbanding to make room for a new team to tackle the next problem. You can feel the continuous cultural motion as groups of people come together to solve a particular problem or challenge, and then separate to join others to solve the next one.

What holds a company together in an environment of relentless flux? What defines a group and enables its members to come together quickly to get work done effectively? Need we say it? *Culture*: agreements about how to get work done, about identity and connection, about leadership, about visions of the future. Culture is not the solution to every challenge, *but it is the source material from which solutions can be drawn.*

As we work with a wide variety of organizations, we are starting to see these solutions take hold, enabling us to make an educated guess about what the future may look like for many companies. We call it the superconducting organization.

The Superconducting Organization

The word "superconducting" may seem jarring in the context of ethnography, folklore, and fine embroidery, but it best describes the kind of organization that avoids the barriers, slowdowns, and silos of the past and builds on its culture to become faster moving, more nimble, and more adaptable. When an organization becomes superconducting, talent, innovation, and change flow swiftly and freely across the enterprise, and the information in resistance becomes a source of feedback and forward energy. In this new paradigm, leadership creates engagement, engagement creates action, and action delivers results. We realize that superconducting is an ideal, an aspiration, a state worth working toward.

We have learned a great deal about the elements of a super-conducting organization through people we work with—in corporations, family businesses, and the nonprofit worlds of health care and universities. Many of them are working diligently to discover new ways of organizing to respond to a radically changed environment in which solutions from the industrial age are no longer relevant.

What is our future? This is a big question with no easy answers. To help you prepare for it, here are three themes that have emerged from our work, practices that many of the people we work with have found useful.

1. Make the Tacit Explicit

Most agreements about how work gets done are tacit, implicit, and undiscussed. Over time, they get taken for granted as the "natural" way to do things. Making them explicit and open for debate and dialogue can transform culture from being fixed and invisible to being accessible and adaptive.

At University Hospital, for example, some of the nurse leaders believed that when Andrea Crowley introduced new ways of working at the bedside with patients, they would have to implement them simply because Crowley, their boss, told them to. Their tacit understanding: command and control is the way things get done around here. Once Crowley demonstrated that this was not about command and control, they could change their assumptions, and what seemed fixed became flexible. What previously could not be talked about became discussable. Her nurse leaders discovered that Crowley wanted nurses to have more time to spend at the bedside with patients—how they put that into practice was open to learning and experimentation. A cultural shift became possible from command and control to command and collaborate—and it took both Crowley and her nurse leaders to make that shift possible. Once the direction for the shift was clear, it was easy to sweep others in and spread new practices that enabled nurses throughout the UH system to spend more time with their patients.

2. Pull, Don't Push

Using the push approach to change generates resistance by slamming into current agreements for getting work done. Pull approaches, on the other hand, attract people who are already working in new ways that, at the same time, fit with the existing culture. When you want to try a new approach to working, always make your first question, *Where is this already happening?* And think about ways to invite people to participate in those new ways of working rather than pushing it on them. Enroll, don't steamroll.

At this very minute, some people somewhere in your organization are doing positively deviant things that are examples of the new organization that is emerging as the old one unravels. Like Dr. Green at University Hospital, they are creatively stretching existing cultural limits in fascinating and creative ways. They are a resource waiting for you to discover them.

As we've seen, listening in for found pilots—then connecting them with each other and supporting them—is a surefire way to learn more about the future you're trying to create as you're creating it, while remaining true to your identity. This is what happened at Quire. When strategy had to shift to meet new competitive demands, the company relied on one of the core components of its culture—Six Sigma—to enroll people in the new strategy.

3. Move Toward Resistance

We create most of the organizational obstacles that stand in our way—and consequently we can and should be the ones who remove them. Working with skeptical friends, for example, is a useful way to locate and then understand the logic behind the resistance that always accompanies change. It often helps to begin with ourselves. As Jerry Harvey, a management scholar, has so wisely observed, "How come every time I get stabbed in the back my fingerprints are on the knife?"[1]

When Kenneth Patterson at Moncrieff University began to run into resistance, he was frustrated. But as he learned to work his way through the resistance, moving toward it rather than away, he came to understand more about how universities work and about the contributions that other people—faculty, staff, board members—could make to the plan he was developing. Our instinct may be to move away from resistance, but in this case instinct does not serve us well.

An Exhortation

We wrote this book because we have met and worked with many leaders who want to understand how to unleash the productive energy of their organizations in pursuit of a new strategic direction. In organization after organization, we have seen that ethnographic methods—listening in to the organization, observing how culture evolves into behavior, and paying attention to the ways that social capital expands when authority is shared—can help leaders guide their organizations through the turbulent process of strategic change.

We have also seen that many leaders, even those who seek to unleash the energy of their organizations, are reluctant to enter into the cultural conversation. There are so many other things that need their attention. Plus, there is risk. When you begin a conversation, you can't be sure how it will go, where it will end, and how it may shake things up. And lurking behind all those concerns is an even more daunting and fundamental set of questions: What will this mean for me? Will I have to change, too? Will I lose my way? Can I succeed? Will I fail?

All these concerns are valid, but the conversations about culture *must eventually be had.* If you choose to ignore your un-ignorable moments, your culture may become fractured and chaotic. Any changes you attempt through means other than unleashing cultural energy will be short-lived at best, and destructive at worst. If you choose to look for the future only *outside* your organization—in "best practices" or ready-made strategies—rather than inside it, you run the risk of discouraging or even destroying the best and most promising parts of your culture. Eventually you will discover that even the best of best practices must fit with your culture if they are to be adopted, spread, and stick. If you try to push people toward change, rather than using pull techniques to sweep them in, you will find that the culture will resist—with good reason—and factions and underground movements will form to preserve the status quo. And if your leaders are unable to tap into the culture to create a coalition of the willing or choose not to, those in charge will likely depart long before the culture even begins to embrace the new—just like many CEOs and university presidents and leaders of other organizations. In other words, whatever approach you may take, *culture will still be there* and it will determine the degree and speed of your success.

Despite our opining about the disintegration of organizational forms and our warnings about potential disasters that await the change maker, we are highly optimistic about the fourth question. We have worked with many leaders who have put into practice the three guiding principles—make the tacit explicit, pull don't push, move toward resistance—and have been able to mine their culture as a renewable resource and make progress along the path to becoming a superconducting organization.

What's more, we believe that collectively we are facing a moment that can't be ignored—the old organizational structures can no longer facilitate or support the work we need to do in the years to come. At the same time, we believe there is fantastic potential in this moment for organizations to create new agreements for engaging and organizing talented people at work, to build on that most sustainable resource—culture—and thus to innovate and grow.

So, our parting exhortation is simple. When your moment arrives, don't ignore it—give it your fullest and most earnest attention.

In your culture you will find your future.

ACKNOWLEDGMENTS

WE ARE GRATEFUL TO THE MANY PEOPLE whose guidance, support and critical thinking have contributed to this book. As we wrote the book, we realized that the way we look at the world has been strongly influenced by a few mentors early in our careers. Ray Birdwhistell taught us how to look at everyday behavior in ways that made what had been so familiar and taken for granted suddenly new and strange enough to pay attention to. It was Ray who helped us understand the difference between psychological and social frames for understanding communication, and the value of both–the difference between searching for a deeper interpretation of actions and events that we participate in out of our awareness, and the information that comes from paying attention to how people act right in front of our eyes.

Henry Glassie, through his fifty-year fascination with the creation of ideas and objects, taught Mal how to be with people, to understand the logic of their experience and the cultural agreements that shape that logic. He is a master of identifying and articulating the tacit rules for interaction in ways that make them clear, explicit, and accessible.

Tom Gilmore, Larry Hirschhorn, Lynn Oppenheim, Joe Ryan, and Mal himself helped Barry make the complicated transition from academia to organizational consulting, and to better understand the different mindsets required and different ways to work in these domains without losing one's identity in the mix. Neil Kleinman taught Barry a great deal about how to navigate organizational life with grace, humor, optimism, and a lot of persistence.

We have been very fortunate to work with engaged and thoughtful clients and the insightful people in the organizations they lead and serve. At the center of every case, story, and unignorable moment we describe, are leaders with whom we have collaborated to develop capabilities their organizations needed in order to remain competitive and thrive. They know through their own experience that learning-how-to-learn, and getting stuck and unstuck along the way, are some of those critical capabilities. And they have helped us get ourselves unstuck many times too. It is our clients who provide the live learning laboratories where, together, we continuously develop our cultural approach to working with and through change.

This is a CFAR book. It emerges out of the unique history and perspective of the firm and our ongoing relationships with our clients. The stories told are those of clients and projects that many of our colleagues at the firm have worked on over the years–and our colleagues contributed to the book in several ways. CFAR's management team, led by our president, Lynn

Oppenheim, supported us from start to finish. Carey Gallagher, Caitlyn Fleming, and Katey Watts worked on every chapter of the book, selecting and exploring project cases, doing research and keeping us on track in order to meet deadlines.

The ideas and method outlined in the book have been developed in collaboration with clients over many years. Our colleagues Tom Gilmore, Larry Hirschhorn and Linda May were early shapers of our cultural approach to leading and managing change, and read sections of the manuscript at different stages to give us their advice. It has been the experience of testing these ideas with our clients that has proven the value of this approach. Nancy Drozdow, Debbie Bing, Jerrel Jones, and Carey Gallagher worked on the family business cases described in the book. Jennifer Tomasik, Lynn Oppenheim, Nat Welch, and Chris Hugill were integral to the healthcare projects. The collective learning from their work informs the ideas throughout the book and fuels the way we continue to work and learn with and from each other.

Many years in the making, this project would not have seen the light of day without the support of the team that made it possible. We thank our guide and collaborator, John Butman, and his colleagues Anna Weiss, Henry Butman, and Barbara Lynn-Davis of Idea Platforms, Inc. John guided us from the start, from his first question, "Do you really have something at all interesting or new to say about change?" through the proposal and the multiple drafts that resulted, finally, in this book. His combination of brutally honest critique and continuous encouragement kept us going through the highs and lows all along the way. We also want to thank Steven Zorn for his

contributions to the Case of A Leader Who Found a New Kind
of Power.

We have had the good fortune to work with terrific agents and
a highly professional and experienced publishing team. Jacob
Moore, and his colleague, Todd Shuster, at Zachary, Shuster,
Harmsworth took us on and then pushed us to sharpen the focus
of our proposal. Their critique helped us clarify our own point
of view, and is one of the reasons we were able to attract the interest of John Mahaney at Public Affairs Books. Our experience
working with John and Public Affairs has been terrific. John
devoted a great deal of time to reading and critiquing the manuscript at several stages of its evolution, and encouraged us to
include the three composite case narratives that, we hope, com-
plement the more traditional idea-based chapters in the book.

We would also like to thank Carole Boughter, Tracy Cox,
Tom Gilmore, Patrick Jordan, Mark Kelley, Bonnie O'Connor,
Mary Beth O'Connor, Don Ronchi, and Pang Xiong Sirirathasuk Sikoun for reading and critiquing specific chapters as we
drafted them. Their experience and insights helped strengthen
those chapters. The remaining errors of commission and omis-
sion are our own.

Finally, each of us would like to thank our family and friends.

Mal: My mother, Tina, a poet and biographer in her own
right, has always encouraged me to take smart risks and let go
of closely held ideas when they just don't work. She is one of
the very few people I have ever met who knows how to embrace
change in the face of the anxiety and fear it sometimes generates.
Very special thanks to my wife, Bonnie O'Connor, who played

multiple roles. In addition to supplying the love and support so much needed throughout the process, Bonnie is a folklorist and scholar who has for twenty-five years taught and trained physicians to understand the cultural agreements at the heart of their interactions with patients, their profession, and with the healthcare system of which they are a part. Her honest feedback and analytical rigor kept me grounded, as she asked one more time, "What does this have to do with culture and how it works?" Our close friends, Rik and Wendi Bourne, Lin Brodsky, and Rob Strauss engaged in endless conversations about ideas along the way, and tolerated my total immersion in the book during weekends we spent together over the past couple of years.

Barry: My wife Carole Boughter has been a constant vitalizing and loving presence in my life and in my work. She listens incisively, brings her unique perspective to my work, and has been an amazing sounding board and champion for me throughout this writing process. She brought to bear her own years of pioneering experience in cultural and organizational work in giving us her feedback and advice. Ted and Maura, our kids, are ongoing sources of love, support, encouragement, and creative energy and joy in our lives. If their pride in me represents even a small proportion of the enormous pride I have in them, I feel rewarded. My mother Ina is a wonderful model of love, intelligence, street smarts, and resilience that I hope I come close to matching. Lastly, Ira Greenberg, Dan Cook, Lisa Henderson, and the late Gene Michaud are fellow travelers in diverging journeys that have brought us somehow to compatible places. I have learned much from their unique minds and great senses of humor over the years.

NOTES

INTRODUCTION: THE MANY WAYS TO ATTEND A FUNERAL

1. The Folklife Center of International House in Philadelphia, led by Carole Boughter, conceived and organized the innovative Hmong Community Folklife and Documentation Project from 1984 to 1985 in collaboration with local Hmong leaders.

2. See Bonnie O'Connor's analysis of the cultural dimensions of Bee's illness and treatment in "Negotiating Clinically Workable Solutions Across Cultures: Lessons Learned," *Medicine and Health Rhode Island,* December 2008, 365–368.

3. Ray L. Birdwhistell, *Kinesics and Context, Essays on Body Motion Communication* (Philadelphia: University of Pennsylvania Press, 1970).

4. Bronislaw Malinowski, *Argonauts of the Western Pacific* (London: Routledge, 1932).

5. There are several excellent guides to participant observation, including: Paul Atkinson and Martyn Hammersley, "Ethnography and Participant Observation," in Norman K. Denzin and Yvonna S. Lincoln, eds., *Handbook of Qualitative Research* (Thousand Oaks, CA: Sage, 1994), 248–261. Kathleen DeWalt and Billie R. De Walt, *Participant Observation: A Guide for Fieldworkers,* 2nd ed. (Plymouth, UK: Altamira, 2010). Stephen L. Schensul, Jean J. Schensuk, and Margaret D. LeCompte, *Essential Ethnographic Methods: Observations, Interviews, and Questionnaires,* vol. 2 of *The Ethnographer's Toolkit,* ed. Jean J. Schensul and Margaret D. LeCompte (Walnut Creek, CA: Altamira, 1999), 91–120. James P. Spradley, *Participant Observation* (New York: Holt, Rinehart & Winston, 1980).

6. There is a long history of ethnographic studies of organizations and business from multiple perspectives and methods. Douglas Caulkins and Ann Jordan summarize these studies in *A Companion to Organizational Anthropology* (Hoboken, NJ: Wiley, 2012). Some examples we have found particularly helpful are Gideon Kunda's ethnography of the culture of a high-tech company in Silicon Valley in *Engineering Culture Control and Commitment in a High-tech Corporation* (Philadelphia: Temple University Press, 2006); and Alexandra Michel's and Stanton Wortham's fascinating look at life in two Wall Street investment banks in *Bullish on Uncertainty: How Organizational Cultures Transform Participants* (New York: Cambridge University Press, 2008). Dornfeld's

book *Producing Public Television, Producing Public Culture* (Princeton, NJ: Princeton University Press, 1998) offers another example of organizational ethnography looking at the production of a public television documentary.

7. Our review of early ethnographies reminded us of the importance of funerals as windows into understanding how a culture works. Franz Boas, for example, a seminal figure in American ethnography, worked extensively with a Northwest Pacific American Indian nation, the Kwakiutl. Boas made the point that if you want to understand a culture's norms for mourning and managing loss, don't watch the funeral. Watch the Kwakiutl watching the funeral. See Franz Boas, *Kwakiutl Ethnography* (Chicago: University of Chicago Press, 1966). For more on Boas and his work with the Kwakiutl, see http://www.mpm.edu/research-collections/artifacts/kwakiutl/ethnography.

2: THE UN-IGNORABLE MOMENT

1. "The End of Merck," *Forbes,* March 10, 2009.

2. "Merck Offers Free Distribution of New River Blindness Drug," *New York Times,* October 22, 1987, http://www.nytimes.com/1987/10/22/world/merck-offers-free-distribution-of-new-river-blindness-drug.html.

3. "Vioxx Taken Off the Market," Harvard Medical School Family Health Guide, December 2004, http://www.health.harvard.edu/fhg/updates/update1204d.shtml.

4. Marcia Angell, *The Truth About the Drug Companies: How They Deceive Us and What to Do About It* (New York: Random House, 2004).

5. Kurt W. Rotthoff, "Product Liability Litigation: An Issue of Merck and Lawsuits over Vioxx," Stillman School of Business, Seton Hall University, January 2009, http://pirate.shu.edu/~rotthoku/papers/Merck.pdf.

6. In an alternate view, Noel Tichy and Warren Bennis focus on leadership more than culture in their valuable interpretation of Merck's struggles with this un-ignorable moment; we see the two as intertwined. Noel Tichy and Warren Bennis, *Judgment: How Winning Leaders Make Great Calls* (New York: Penguin, 2007).

7. Edgar H. Schein, *Organizational Culture and Leadership,* 4th ed. (San Francisco: Jossey-Bass, 2010); Schein, *The Corporate Culture Survival Guide* (San Francisco: Jossey-Bass, 2009); Schein, *Organizational Culture: A Dynamic Model* (Cambridge: Alfred P. Sloan School of Management, Massachusetts Institute of Technology, 1983), http://archive.org/details/organizationalcu00sche.

8. John P. Kotter and James L. Heskett, *Corporate Culture and Performance* (New York: Free Press, 2011).

9. Edgar H. Schein, *DEC Is Dead, Long Live DEC: The Lasting Legacy of Digital Equipment Corporation* (San Francisco: Berrett-Koehler, 2004).

10. Peter Brush, "The Hard Truth About Fragging," July 28, 2010, http://www.historynet.com/the-hard-truth-about-fragging.htm.

11. Ibid.

12. Ibid.

13. Michael Fullan, *Leading in a Culture of Change* (San Francisco: Jossey-Bass, 2001).

14. Nancy M. Dixon, *Common Knowledge: How Companies Thrive by sharing What They Know.* (Boston: Harvard Business, 2000). Marilyn Darling, Charles Parry, and

Joseph Moore, "Learning in the Thick of It," *Harvard Business Review,* July 2005.

15. James Spradley, well-known as a pioneer in participant observation techniques, discusses the value of making the tacit explicit in *Participant Observation* (New York: Holt, Rinehart & Winston, 1980).

16. "DMAIC: The 5 Phases of Lean Six Sigma," http://www.goleansixsigma.com /dmaic-five-basic-phases-of-lean-six-sigma.

17. Clifford Geertz, *The Interpretation of Cultures: Selected Essays* (New York: Basic, 1973).

18. Ibid., 3–30. In his essay, "Thick Description: Toward an Interpretive Theory of Culture," Geertz outlines the meaning of thick description and its connection to interpretation of cultural experience during fieldwork.

3: A CASE OF ADAPTIVE IDENTITY

1. Nancy M. Dixon, "The Changing Face of Knowledge," *Learning Organization* 6, no. 5 (1999): 212–216.

2. Jon R. Katzenbach, Ilona Steffen, and Caroline Kronley, "Cultural Change That Sticks," *Harvard Business Review,* July–August 2012.

4: FINDING THE FUTURE INSIDE

1. William Gibson, the well-known science fiction writer, is reported to have made this statement, often cited but difficult to attribute with precision.

2. D. W. Winnicott, "Transitional Objects and Transitional Phenomena: A Study of the First Not-me Possession," *International Journal of Psychoanalysis* 34 (1953): 89–97.

3. Open-source Cancer Research, 2014, http://www.ted.com/talks/jay_bradner _open_source_cancer_research.html.

4. Kevin Dunbar, "What Scientific Thinking Reveals About the Nature of Cognition," in Kevin Crowley, Christian D. Schunn, and Takeshi Okada, eds., *Designing for Science: Implications from Everyday, Classroom, and Professional Settings* (London: Psychology Press, 2001), 461.

5. Ray Oldenburg, *The Great Good Place: Cafés, Coffee Shop Bookstores, Bars, Hair Salons, and Other Hangouts at the Heart of a Community* (Cambridge, MA: Da Capo, 1999).

6. Steven Johnson, *Where Good Ideas Come From: The Natural History of Innovation* (New York: Riverhead, 2010).

7. Greg Lindsay, "Coworking Spaces from Grind to Grid70 Help Employees Work Beyond the Cube," *Fast Company,* March 2013, http://www.fastcompany .com/3004915/coworking-nextspace.

8. Alan Feuer, "The Man with a Plan to Rebuild After the Apocalypse," *New York Times,* March 16, 2012, http://www.nytimes.com/2012/03/18/nyregion/the-man-with-a-plan -to-rebuild-after-the-apocalypse.html.

9. Claude Lévi-Strauss, *The Savage Mind* (Chicago: University of Chicago Press, 1966).

10. Marian Zeitlin et al., *Positive Deviance in Child Nutrition* (New York: United Nations University, 1990).

11. Richard T. Pascale, Jerry Sternin, and Monique Sternin, *The Power of Positive Deviance: How Improbable Innovators Solve the World's Toughest Problems* (Boston: Harvard Business Press, 2010).

12. See John Kotter, *Building Strategic Agility for a Faster-Moving World,* and John Hagel, John Seely Brown, and Lang Davison, *The Power of Pull: How Small Moves, Smartly Made, Can Set Big Things in Motion* (New York: Basic, 2010).

13. Malcolm Gladwell, "The Coolhunt," *New Yorker,* March 17, 1997, http://www.newyorker.com/archive/1997/03/17/1997_03_17_078_TNY_CARDS_000378002.

14. Jon R. Katzenbach, Ilona Steffen, and Caroline Kronley, "Cultural Change That Sticks," *Harvard Business Review,* July–August 2012.

5: SWEEPING PEOPLE IN

1. There are many definitions of social capital and a great deal of research focuses on how to build it. People who have social capital can exert influence through their networks to introduce, recommend, and support new behaviors and ways of working within an organization. Pierre Bourdieu distinguishes between economic capital, cultural capital, and social capital. He defines social capital as "the aggregate of the actual or potential resources which are linked to possession of a durable network of more or less institutionalized relationships of mutual acquaintance and recognition." Bourdieu, "The Forms of Capital," in *Handbook of Theory and Research for the Sociology of Education,* ed. John Richardson (New York: Greenwood, 1986), 241–258. See also Ronald S. Burt, *Brokerage and Closure: An Introduction to Social Capital* (New York: Oxford University Press, 2005).

2. "Influence," http://www.merriam-webster.com/dictionary/influence.

3. Ronald S. Burt, *Brokerage and Closure: An Introduction to Social Capital* (New York: Oxford University Press, 2005). Ronald S. Burt and Don Ronchi, "Teaching Executives to See Social Capital: Results from a Field Experiment," *Social Science Research* 36, no. 3 (September 2007): 1156–1183. Mark Granovetter, "The Strength of Weak Ties," *American Journal of Sociology* 78, no. 6 (May 1973): 1360–1380. Stephen P. Borgatti and Pacey C. Foster, "The Network Paradigm in Organizational Research: A Review and Typology," *Journal of Management* 26, no. 6 (2003): 991–1013. Stephen P. Borgatti, Ajay Mehra, Daniel J. Brass, and Guiseppe Labianca, "Network Analysis in the Social Sciences," *Science* 323 (2009): 892–895. Robert L. Cross and Robert J. Thomas, *Driving Results Through Social Networks: How Top Organizations Leverage Networks for Performance and Growth* (San Francisco: Jossey-Bass, 2009).

4. For a great study of boundary spanning, consider Brendan Duddy, the owner of a fish and chip shop who served as a go-between for the IRA and the British state during the Northern Ireland peace process. See *The Secret Peacemaker,* BBC Video, 2008.

5. Social network analysis has a long history in the social sciences, and it has been put to productive use in business contexts by several thinkers. Rob Cross at the University of Virginia has applied this tool to making large-scale change work and helping develop organizations more broadly. See Rob Cross, Michael Johnson-Cramer, and Salvatore Parise, "Managing Change through Networks and Values: How a Relational View of Culture Can Facilitate Large-Scale Change," Network Roundtable at the University of Virginia, n.d., http://www.robcross.org/pdf/roundtable/change_through_networks_and_culture.pdf. Rob Cross and Jon Katzenbach, "The Right Role for Top Teams," http://www.strategy-business.com/article/00103?gko=97c39. Margaret Schweer, Dimitris Assimakopoulos, Rob Cross,

and Robert J. Thomas, "Building a Well-Networked Organization," *MIT Sloan Management Review,* http://sloanreview.mit.edu/article/building-a-well-networked-organization.

6. G. Richard Shell and Mario Moussa, *The Art of Woo: Using Strategic Persuasion to Sell Your Ideas* (New York: Penguin, 2008).

7. Robert B. Cialdini, *Influence: The Psychology of Persuasion* (New York: Collins, 2007).

8. Marcel Mauss and W. D. Halls, *The Gift: The Form and Reason for Exchange in Archaic Societies* (New York: Norton, 1990).

6: THE CASE OF A LEADER WHO FINDS A NEW KIND OF POWER

1. A fairly extensive literature exists on presidential transitions and failures in higher education, including Stephen Joel Trachtenberg, Gerald B. Kauvar, and E. Grady Bogue, *Presidencies Derailed: Why University Leaders Fail and How to Prevent It* (Baltimore: Johns Hopkins University Press, 2013); and Patrick Sanaghan, *Presidential Transitions: It's Not Just the Position, It's the Transition* (Westport, CT: Praeger Trade, 2008).

7: LEADING LEADERS

1. The notion of loosely coupled systems is often attributed to organizational theorist Karl Weick, who described educational organizations as "loosely coupled" in "Educational Organizations as Loosely Coupled Systems," *Administrative Science Quarterly* 21 (1976): 1–19.

2. For more on ways in which turbulence increases the need for collaboration across organizational boundaries, see Fred Emery and E. L. Trist Emery, *Towards a Social Ecology: Contextual Appreciations of the Future in the Present* (New York: Plenum, 1973). An updated treatment of these issues can be found in Mal O'Connor and Tom Gilmore's unpublished paper, "Use of Design to Advance Collaborations Among Multiple Organizations with Strong Professional Identities," presented at the ISPSO Symposium in June 2013.

3. Richard Norman and Rafael Ramirez, *Designing Interactive Strategy: From Value Chain to Value Constellation* (New York: Wiley, 2005).

4. Liz Wiseman, *Multipliers: How the Best Leaders Make Everyone Smarter* (New York: HarperCollins, 2011).

5. John Hagel, John Seely Brown, and Lang Davison, *The Power of Pull: How Small Moves, Smartly Made, Can Set Big Things in Motion* (New York: Basic, 2010).

6. Choice theory in behavioral economics and psychology explores similar terrain in which researchers look at how to encourage certain kinds of choices through the use of default options and other ways to create "pull." See, for instance, Barry Schwartz, *The Paradox of Choice: Why More Is Less* (New York: Ecco, 2004).

7. Cialdini, *Influence.* Barry M. Staw, "Knee-Deep in the Big Muddy: A Study of Escalating Commitment to a Chosen Course of Action," *Organizational Behavior and Human Performance* 16, no. 1 (1976): 27–44.

8. Our colleague Larry Hirschhorn foresaw the coming of this new work environment in *Managing in the New Team Environment: Skills, Tools, and Methods* (Lincoln, NE: Authors Choice Press, 2002).

9. Daniel Pink summarizes research on motivation and its application to the work

environment in his recent book *Drive: The Surprising Truth About What Motivates Us* (New York: Riverhead, 2011).

10. Abraham Maslow, "A Theory of Human Motivation," *Psychology Review* 50, no. 4 (July 1943): 370–396.

11. Richard H. Thaler and Cass R. Sunstein, *Nudge: Improving Decisions About Health, Wealth, and Happiness* (New York: Penguin, 2009).

12. Dan Ariely, *Predictably Irrational: The Hidden Forces That Shape Our Decisions* (New York: Harper Perennial, 2010).

13. Pink, *Drive*.

14. Ibid.

CONCLUSION: WHAT IS OUR FUTURE?

1. Jerry B. Harvey, *How Come Every Time I Get Stabbed in the Back My Fingerprints Are on the Knife? And Other Meditations on Management* (San Francisco: Jossey-Bass, 1999).

INDEX

faculty leadership in universities, 218, 222
and followers, 237
leadership development initiatives, 60–61
leading leaders, 12, 215, 223, 232, 233, 239, 240, 241
and motivating people, 215
new, 192
primary tasks of, 223
sharing leadership, 221, 222, 223–224, 231, 232–233, 254
and shift from push to pull, 234
skills needed for, 248
and social capital, 159–160
team-based approach to, 222
and tightly/loosely coupled organizations, 215, 217, 219–223, 237, 239, 240, 241
and workforce, 213
See also Organizations: and leadership/authority issues
Lean method, 58
Levi-Strauss, Claude, 137
'Listening in' process, 8, 18–19, 25, 34, 38, 75–78, 79, 105, 131, 140, 144, 149, 151, 186, 227, 252, 254
listening to opposition, 162
Lor, Bee 1, 3–4, 10, 245
Loyalty, 214, 225, 233

McGlynn, Sheri, 23, 34–38, 43–44, 80
Macleish, Inc., 49–51
Madagascar Institute, 137
MADD. *See* Mothers Against Drunk Driving
Malinowski, Bronislaw, 5
Management/managers, 225, 226–227, 229, 240
management development support, 73
middle managers, 134–136, 142
Mancuso, Kevin, 227, 229, 230, 231
Mansfield, Mike, 55
Marshfield, Amy, 179–181, 182, 183
Maslow, Abraham, 238

Mathias, Charles, 55
Mauss, Marcel, 166
Mead, Margaret, 168
Medicare Quality Reporting program, 26
Meetings, 72, 88–94, 101, 105, 107, 113–115, 121–124, 125, 126, 136, 164, 169, 182–183, 185–186, 187–190, 190–193, 198, 199, 204–206, 209–211
breakthroughs occurring during, 134
Merck company, 52–54
Mextizan, 52
Miller, Gus, 97–105, 106, 109–110, 111, 113, 115, 116, 159, 160–161, 169, 234, 241
Mission statements, 157, 158
Molecular biologists, 134
Moncrieff University, 179–211, 218–219, 238, 242, 253
faculty's objection to the China project, 197–198
Moncrieff Center for Innovation, 181–182, 183, 187, 193, 197–198, 201, 207, 209, 234, 243
soul of, 189, 198, 202–203, 207–208, 210, 211, 243
See also Board of trustees
Morale of employees, 135
Mothers Against Drunk Driving (MADD), 235
Motivation, 214, 215, 237–239, 242
Motorola, 58
Murphy, Dan, 64–68, 151
Murphy Development, 64–68, 130–132, 151
Murphy Challenge, 131, 132

National Institutes of Health (NIH), 169
Native's point of view, 5, 12. *See also* Participant observation
Natural resources, 54–55
New England Journal of Medicine, 26
NIH. *See* National Institutes of Health
Norris, Jill, 96, 163
Nutrition, 138–139